HBR's 10 Must Reads

UPDATED &
EXPANDED

Strategy

T0418101

HBR's 10 Must Reads

HBR's 10 Must Reads are definitive collections of classic ideas, practical advice, and essential thinking from the pages of *Harvard Business Review*. Exploring topics like disruptive innovation, emotional intelligence, and new technology in our ever-evolving world, these books empower any leader to make bold decisions and inspire others.

TITLES INCLUDE:

HBR's 10 Must Reads for New Managers
HBR's 10 Must Reads on AI
HBR's 10 Must Reads on Building a Great Culture
HBR's 10 Must Reads on Change Management
HBR's 10 Must Reads on Communication
HBR's 10 Must Reads on Data Strategy
HBR's 10 Must Reads on Decision-Making
HBR's 10 Must Reads on Design Thinking
HBR's 10 Must Reads on Digital Transformation
HBR's 10 Must Reads on Emotional Intelligence
HBR's 10 Must Reads on High Performance
HBR's 10 Must Reads on Innovation
HBR's 10 Must Reads on Leadership
HBR's 10 Must Reads on Leading Winning Teams
HBR's 10 Must Reads on Managing People
HBR's 10 Must Reads on Managing Yourself
HBR's 10 Must Reads on Marketing
HBR's 10 Must Reads on Mental Toughness
HBR's 10 Must Reads on Strategy
HBR's 10 Must Reads on Women and Leadership
HBR's 10 Must Reads Boxed Set (6 Books)
HBR's 10 Must Reads Ultimate Boxed Set (14 Books)

For a full list, visit hbr.org/mustreads.

UPDATED &
EXPANDED

Strategy

Harvard Business Review Press
Boston, Massachusetts

Copyright 2025 Harvard Business School Publishing Corporation

All rights reserved

Printed in the United States of America

10 9 8 7 6 5 4 3 2 1

No part of this publication may be reproduced, stored in or introduced into a retrieval system, or transmitted, in any form, or by any means (electronic, mechanical, photocopying, recording, or otherwise), without the prior permission of the publisher. Requests for permission should be directed to permissions@harvardbusiness.org or mailed to Permissions, Harvard Business School Publishing, 60 Harvard Way, Boston, Massachusetts 02163.

The web addresses referenced in this book were live and correct at the time of the book's publication but may be subject to change.

Cataloging-in-Publication data is forthcoming.

ISBN: 979-8-89279-173-1
eISBN: 979-8-89279-174-8

The paper used in this publication meets the requirements of the American National Standard for Permanence of Paper for Publications and Documents in Libraries and Archives Z39.48-1992.

Contents

UPDATED &
EXPANDED

Strategy

The Five Competitive Forces That Shape Strategy

by Michael E. Porter

n essence, the job of the strategist is to understand and cope with competition. Often, however, managers define competition too narrowly, as if it occurred only among today's direct competitors. Yet competition for profits goes beyond established industry rivals to include four other competitive forces as well: customers, suppliers, potential entrants, and substitute products. The extended rivalry that results from all five forces defines an industry's structure and shapes the nature of competitive interaction within an industry.

As different from one another as industries might appear on the surface, the underlying drivers of profitability are the same. The global auto industry, for instance, appears to have nothing in common with the worldwide market for art masterpieces or

The five forces that shape industry competition

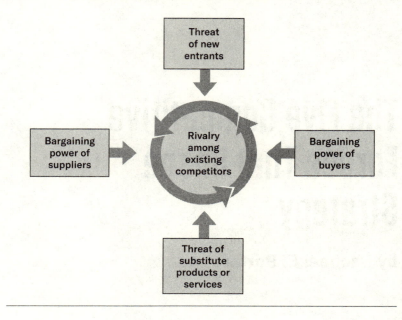

the heavily regulated health-care delivery industry in Europe. But to understand industry competition and profitability in each of those three cases, one must analyze the industry's underlying structure in terms of the five forces. (See the exhibit "The five forces that shape industry competition.")

If the forces are intense, as they are in such industries as airlines, textiles, and hotels, almost no company earns attractive returns on investment. If the forces are benign, as they are in industries such as software, soft drinks, and toiletries, many companies are profitable. Industry structure drives competition and profitability, not whether an industry produces a product or service, is emerging or mature, high tech or low tech, regulated

Idea in Brief

You know that to sustain long-term profitability you must respond strategically to competition. And you naturally keep tabs on your established rivals. But as you scan the competitive arena, are you also looking beyond your direct competitors? As Porter explains in this update of his revolutionary 1979 HBR article, four additional competitive forces can hurt your prospective profits:

- Savvy customers can force down prices by playing you and your rivals against one another.

- Powerful suppliers may constrain your profits if they charge higher prices.

- Aspiring entrants, armed with new capacity and hungry for market share, can ratchet up the investment required for you to stay in the game.

- Substitute offerings can lure customers away.

Consider commercial aviation: It's one of the least profitable industries because all five forces are strong. Established rivals compete intensely on price. Customers are fickle, searching for the best deal regardless of carrier. Suppliers—plane and engine manufacturers, along with unionized labor forces—bargain away the lion's share of airlines' profits. New players enter the industry in a constant stream. And substitutes are readily available—such as train or car travel.

By analyzing all five competitive forces, you gain a complete picture of what's influencing profitability in your industry. You identify game-changing trends early, so you can swiftly exploit them. And you spot ways to work around constraints on profitability—or even reshape the forces in your favor.

or unregulated. While a myriad of factors can affect industry profitability in the short run—including the weather and the business cycle—industry structure, manifested in the competitive forces, sets industry profitability in the medium and long run. (See the exhibit "Differences in industry profitability.")

Differences in Industry Profitability

The average return on invested capital varies markedly from industry to industry. Between 1992 and 2006, for example, average return on invested capital in U.S. industries ranged as low as zero or even negative to more than 50%. At the high end are industries like soft drinks and prepackaged software, which have been almost six times more profitable than the airline industry over the period.

Average return on invested capital in U.S. industries, 1992–2006

Return on invested capital (ROIC) *is the appropriate measure of profitability for strategy formulation, not to mention for equity investors. Return on sales or the growth rate of profits fail to account for the capital required to compete in the industry. Here, we utilize earnings before interest and taxes divided by average invested capital less excess cash as the measure of ROIC. This measure controls for idiosyncratic differences in capital structure and tax rates across companies and industries.*

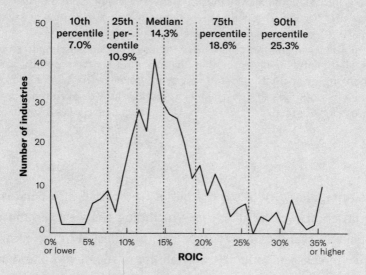

Source: Standard & Poor's, Compustat, and author's calculations

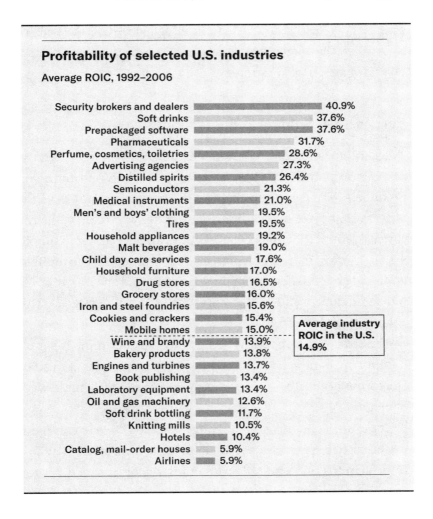

Profitability of selected U.S. industries

Average ROIC, 1992–2006

Security brokers and dealers	40.9%
Soft drinks	37.6%
Prepackaged software	37.6%
Pharmaceuticals	31.7%
Perfume, cosmetics, toiletries	28.6%
Advertising agencies	27.3%
Distilled spirits	26.4%
Semiconductors	21.3%
Medical instruments	21.0%
Men's and boys' clothing	19.5%
Tires	19.5%
Household appliances	19.2%
Malt beverages	19.0%
Child day care services	17.6%
Household furniture	17.0%
Drug stores	16.5%
Grocery stores	16.0%
Iron and steel foundries	15.6%
Cookies and crackers	15.4%
Mobile homes	15.0%
Wine and brandy	13.9%
Bakery products	13.8%
Engines and turbines	13.7%
Book publishing	13.4%
Laboratory equipment	13.4%
Oil and gas machinery	12.6%
Soft drink bottling	11.7%
Knitting mills	10.5%
Hotels	10.4%
Catalog, mail-order houses	5.9%
Airlines	5.9%

Average industry ROIC in the U.S. 14.9%

Understanding the competitive forces, and their underlying causes, reveals the roots of an industry's current profitability while providing a framework for anticipating and influencing competition (and profitability) over time. A healthy industry structure should be as much a competitive concern to strategists as their company's own position. Understanding industry structure is also essential to effective strategic positioning. As we will see, defending against the competitive forces and shaping them in a company's favor are crucial to strategy.

Forces That Shape Competition

The configuration of the five forces differs by industry. In the market for commercial aircraft, fierce rivalry between dominant producers Airbus and Boeing and the bargaining power of the airlines that place huge orders for aircraft are strong, while the threat of entry, the threat of substitutes, and the power of suppliers are more benign. In the movie theater industry, the proliferation of substitute forms of entertainment and the power of the movie producers and distributors who supply movies, the critical input, are important.

The strongest competitive force or forces determine the profitability of an industry and become the most important to strategy formulation. The most salient force, however, is not always obvious.

For example, even though rivalry is often fierce in commodity industries, it may not be the factor limiting profitability. Low returns in the photographic film industry, for instance, are the result of a superior substitute product—as Kodak and Fuji, the world's leading producers of photographic film, learned with the advent of digital photography. In such a situation, coping with the substitute product becomes the number one strategic priority.

Industry structure grows out of a set of economic and technical characteristics that determine the strength of each competitive force. We will examine these drivers in the pages that follow, taking the perspective of an incumbent, or a company already

Industry Analysis in Practice

Good industry analysis looks rigorously at the structural underpinnings of profitability. A first step is to understand the appropriate time horizon. One of the essential tasks in industry analysis is to distinguish temporary or cyclical changes from structural changes. A good guideline for the appropriate time horizon is the full business cycle for the particular industry. For most industries, a three-to-five-year horizon is appropriate, although in some industries with long lead times, such as mining, the appropriate horizon might be a decade or more. It is average profitability over this period, not profitability in any particular year, that should be the focus of analysis.

The point of industry analysis is not to declare the industry attractive or unattractive but to understand the underpinnings of competition and the root causes of profitability. As much as possible, analysts should look at industry structure quantitatively, rather than be satisfied with lists of qualitative factors. Many elements of the five forces can be quantified: the percentage of the buyer's total cost accounted for by the industry's product (to understand buyer price sensitivity); the percentage of industry sales required to fill a plant or operate a logistical network of efficient scale (to help assess barriers to entry); the buyer's switching cost (determining the inducement an entrant or rival must offer customers).

The strength of the competitive forces affects prices, costs, and the investment required to compete; thus the forces are directly tied to the income statements and balance sheets of industry participants. Industry structure defines the gap between revenues and costs. For example, intense rivalry drives down prices or elevates the costs of marketing, R&D, or customer service, reducing margins. How much? Strong suppliers drive up input costs. How much? Buyer power lowers prices or elevates the costs of meeting buyers' demands, such as the requirement to hold more inventory or provide financing. How much? Low barriers to entry or close substitutes limit the level of sustainable prices. How much? It is these economic relationships that sharpen the strategist's understanding of industry competition.

(continued)

> ## Industry Analysis in Practice (*continued*)
>
> Finally, good industry analysis does not just list pluses and minuses but sees an industry in overall systemic terms. Which forces are underpinning (or constraining) today's profitability? How might shifts in one competitive force trigger reactions in others? Answering such questions is often the source of true strategic insights.

present in the industry. The analysis can be readily extended to understand the challenges facing a potential entrant.

Threat of entry

New entrants to an industry bring new capacity and a desire to gain market share that puts pressure on prices, costs, and the rate of investment necessary to compete. Particularly when new entrants are diversifying from other markets, they can leverage existing capabilities and cash flows to shake up competition, as Pepsi did when it entered the bottled water industry, Microsoft did when it began to offer internet browsers, and Apple did when it entered the music distribution business.

The threat of entry, therefore, puts a cap on the profit potential of an industry. When the threat is high, incumbents must hold down their prices or boost investment to deter new competitors. In specialty coffee retailing, for example, relatively low entry barriers mean that Starbucks must invest aggressively in modernizing stores and menus.

The threat of entry in an industry depends on the height of entry barriers that are present and on the reaction entrants can expect from incumbents. If entry barriers are low and newcomers expect little retaliation from the entrenched competitors, the threat of entry is high and industry profitability is moderated. It is the *threat* of entry, not whether entry actually occurs, that holds down profitability.

Barriers to entry. Entry barriers are advantages that incumbents have relative to new entrants. There are seven major sources:

1. *Supply-side economies of scale.* These economies arise when firms that produce at larger volumes enjoy lower costs per unit because they can spread fixed costs over more units, employ more efficient technology, or command better terms from suppliers. Supply-side scale economies deter entry by forcing the aspiring entrant either to come into the industry on a large scale, which requires dislodging entrenched competitors, or to accept a cost disadvantage.

   Scale economies can be found in virtually every activity in the value chain; which ones are most important varies by industry. In microprocessors, incumbents such as Intel are protected by scale economies in research, chip fabrication, and consumer marketing. For lawn care companies like Scotts Miracle-Gro, the most important scale economies are found in the supply chain and media advertising. In small-package delivery, economies of scale arise in national logistical systems and information technology.

2. *Demand-side benefits of scale.* These benefits, also known as network effects, arise in industries where a buyer's willingness to pay for a company's product increases with the number of other buyers who also patronize the company. Buyers may trust larger companies more for a crucial product: Recall the old adage that no one ever got fired

for buying from IBM (when it was the dominant computer maker). Buyers may also value being in a "network" with a larger number of fellow customers. For instance, online auction participants are attracted to eBay because it offers the most potential trading partners. Demand-side benefits of scale discourage entry by limiting the willingness of customers to buy from a newcomer and by reducing the price the newcomer can command until it builds up a large base of customers.

3. *Customer switching costs.* Switching costs are fixed costs that buyers face when they change suppliers. Such costs may arise because a buyer who switches vendors must, for example, alter product specifications, retrain employees to use a new product, or modify processes or information systems. The larger the switching costs, the harder it will be for an entrant to gain customers. Enterprise resource planning (ERP) software is an example of a product with very high switching costs. Once a company has installed SAP's ERP system, for example, the costs of moving to a new vendor are astronomical because of embedded data, the fact that internal processes have been adapted to SAP, major retraining needs, and the mission-critical nature of the applications.

4. *Capital requirements.* The need to invest large financial resources in order to compete can deter new entrants. Capital may be necessary not only for fixed facilities but also to extend customer credit, build inventories, and fund start-up losses. The barrier is particularly great if the capital is required for unrecoverable and therefore harder-to-finance expenditures, such as up-front advertising or research and

development. While major corporations have the financial resources to invade almost any industry, the huge capital requirements in certain fields limit the pool of likely entrants. Conversely, in such fields as tax preparation services or short-haul trucking, capital requirements are minimal and potential entrants plentiful.

It is important not to overstate the degree to which capital requirements alone deter entry. If industry returns are attractive and are expected to remain so, and if capital markets are efficient, investors will provide entrants with the funds they need. For aspiring air carriers, for instance, financing is available to purchase expensive aircraft because of their high resale value—one reason why there have been numerous new airlines in almost every region.

5. *Incumbency advantages independent of size.* No matter what their size, incumbents may have cost or quality advantages not available to potential rivals. These advantages can stem from such sources as proprietary technology, preferential access to the best raw material sources, preemption of the most favorable geographic locations, established brand identities, or cumulative experience that has allowed incumbents to learn how to produce more efficiently. Entrants try to bypass such advantages. Upstart discounters such as Target and Walmart, for example, have located stores in freestanding sites rather than regional shopping centers, where established department stores were well entrenched.

6. *Unequal access to distribution channels.* The new entrant must, of course, secure distribution of its product or service.

A new food item, for example, must displace others from the supermarket shelf via price breaks, promotions, intense selling efforts, or some other means. The more limited the wholesale or retail channels are and the more that existing competitors have tied them up, the tougher entry into an industry will be. Sometimes access to distribution is so high a barrier that new entrants must bypass distribution channels altogether or create their own. Thus, upstart low-cost airlines have avoided distribution through travel agents (who tend to favor established higher-fare carriers) and have encouraged passengers to book their own flights on the internet.

7. *Restrictive government policy.* Government policy can hinder or aid new entry directly, as well as amplify (or nullify) the other entry barriers. Government directly limits or even forecloses entry into industries through, for instance, licensing requirements and restrictions on foreign investment. Regulated industries like liquor retailing, taxi services, and airlines are visible examples. Government policy can heighten other entry barriers through such means as expansive patenting rules that protect proprietary technology from imitation, or environmental or safety regulations that raise scale economies facing newcomers. Of course, government policies may also make entry easier—directly through subsidies, for instance, or indirectly by funding basic research and making it available to all firms, new and old, reducing scale economies.

Entry barriers should be assessed relative to the capabilities of potential entrants, which may be startups, foreign firms, or companies in related industries. And as some of our examples illustrate, the strategist must be mindful of the creative ways newcomers might find to circumvent apparent barriers.

Expected retaliation. How potential entrants believe incumbents may react will also influence their decision to enter or stay out of an industry. If reaction is vigorous and protracted enough, the profit potential of participating in the industry can fall below the cost of capital. Incumbents often use public statements and responses to one entrant to send a message to other prospective entrants about their commitment to defending market share.

Newcomers are likely to fear expected retaliation if:

- Incumbents have previously responded vigorously to new entrants.

- Incumbents possess substantial resources to fight back, including excess cash and unused borrowing power, available productive capacity, or clout with distribution channels and customers.

- Incumbents seem likely to cut prices because they are committed to retaining market share at all costs or because the industry has high fixed costs, which create a strong motivation to drop prices to fill excess capacity.

- Industry growth is slow so newcomers can gain volume only by taking it from incumbents.

An analysis of barriers to entry and expected retaliation is obviously crucial for any company contemplating entry into a new industry. The challenge is to find ways to surmount the entry barriers without nullifying, through heavy investment, the profitability of participating in the industry.

The power of suppliers

Powerful suppliers capture more of the value for themselves by charging higher prices, limiting quality or services, or shifting costs to industry participants. Powerful suppliers, including suppliers of labor, can squeeze profitability out of an industry that is unable to pass on cost increases in its own prices. Microsoft, for instance, has contributed to the erosion of profitability among personal computer makers by raising prices on operating systems. PC makers, competing fiercely for customers who can easily switch among them, have limited freedom to raise their prices accordingly.

Companies depend on a wide range of different supplier groups for inputs. A supplier group is powerful if:

- It is more concentrated than the industry it sells to. Microsoft's near monopoly in operating systems, coupled with the fragmentation of PC assemblers, exemplifies this situation.

- The supplier group does not depend heavily on the industry for its revenues. Suppliers serving many industries will not hesitate to extract maximum profits from each one. If a particular industry accounts for a large portion of a supplier group's volume or profit, however, suppliers will want to protect the industry through reasonable pricing and assist in activities such as R&D and lobbying.

- Industry participants face switching costs in changing suppliers. For example, shifting suppliers is difficult if companies have invested heavily in specialized ancillary equipment or in learning how to operate a supplier's equipment (as with Bloomberg terminals used by financial professionals). Or firms may have located their production lines adjacent to a supplier's manufacturing facilities (as in the case of some beverage companies and container manufacturers). When switching costs are high, industry participants find it hard to play suppliers off against one another. (Note that suppliers may have switching costs as well. This limits their power.)

- Suppliers offer products that are differentiated. Pharmaceutical companies that offer patented drugs with distinctive medical benefits have more power over hospitals, health maintenance organizations, and other drug buyers, for example, than drug companies offering me-too or generic products.

- There is no substitute for what the supplier group provides. Pilots' unions, for example, exercise considerable supplier power over airlines partly because there is no good alternative to a well-trained pilot in the cockpit.

- The supplier group can credibly threaten to integrate forward into the industry. In that case, if industry participants make too much money relative to suppliers, they will induce suppliers to enter the market.

The power of buyers

Powerful customers—the flip side of powerful suppliers—can capture more value by forcing down prices, demanding better quality or more service (thereby driving up costs), and generally playing industry participants off against one another, all at the expense of industry profitability. Buyers are powerful if they have negotiating leverage relative to industry participants, especially if they are price sensitive, using their clout primarily to pressure price reductions.

As with suppliers, there may be distinct groups of customers who differ in bargaining power. A customer group has negotiating leverage if:

- There are few buyers, or each one purchases in volumes that are large relative to the size of a single vendor. Large-volume buyers are particularly powerful in industries with high fixed costs, such as telecommunications equipment, offshore drilling, and bulk chemicals. High fixed costs and low marginal costs amplify the pressure on rivals to keep capacity filled through discounting.

- The industry's products are standardized or undifferentiated. If buyers believe they can always find an equivalent product, they tend to play one vendor against another.

- Buyers face few switching costs in changing vendors.

- Buyers can credibly threaten to integrate backward and produce the industry's product themselves if vendors are too profitable. Producers of soft drinks and beer have long controlled the power of packaging manufacturers by threatening to make, and at times actually making, packaging materials themselves.

A buyer group is price sensitive if:

- The product it purchases from the industry represents a significant fraction of its cost structure or procurement budget. Here buyers are likely to shop around and bargain hard, as consumers do for home mortgages. Where the product sold by an industry is a small fraction of buyers' costs or expenditures, buyers are usually less price sensitive.

- The buyer group earns low profits, is strapped for cash, or is otherwise under pressure to trim its purchasing costs. Highly profitable or cash-rich customers, in contrast, are generally less price sensitive (that is, of course, if the item does not represent a large fraction of their costs).

- The quality of buyers' products or services is little affected by the industry's product. Where quality is very much affected by the industry's product, buyers are generally less price sensitive. When purchasing or renting production-quality cameras, for instance, makers of major motion pictures opt for highly reliable equipment with the latest features. They pay limited attention to price.

- The industry's product has little effect on the buyer's other costs. Here, buyers focus on price. Conversely, where an industry's product or service can pay for itself many times over by improving performance or reducing labor, material, or other costs, buyers are usually more interested in quality than in price. Examples include products and services like tax accounting or well logging (which measures below-ground conditions of oil wells) that can save or even make the buyer money. Similarly, buyers tend not to be price sensitive in services such as investment banking, where poor performance can be costly and embarrassing.

Most sources of buyer power apply equally to consumers and to business-to-business customers. Like industrial customers, consumers tend to be more price sensitive if they are purchasing products that are undifferentiated, expensive relative to their incomes, and of a sort where product performance has limited consequences. The major difference with consumers is that their needs can be more intangible and harder to quantify.

Intermediate customers, or customers who purchase the product but are not the end user (such as assemblers or distribution channels), can be analyzed the same way as other buyers, with one important addition. Intermediate customers gain significant bargaining power when they can influence the purchasing decisions of customers downstream. Consumer electronics retailers, jewelry retailers, and agricultural-equipment distributors are examples of distribution channels that exert a strong influence on end customers.

Producers often attempt to diminish channel clout through exclusive arrangements with particular distributors or retailers or by marketing directly to end users. Component manufacturers seek to develop power over assemblers by creating preferences for their components with downstream customers. Such is the case with bicycle parts and with sweeteners. DuPont has created enormous clout by advertising its Stainmaster brand of carpet fibers not only to the carpet manufacturers that actually buy them but also to downstream consumers. Many consumers request Stainmaster carpet even though DuPont is not a carpet manufacturer.

The threat of substitutes

A substitute performs the same or a similar function as an industry's product by a different means. Videoconferencing is a substitute for travel. Plastic is a substitute for aluminum. Email is a substitute for express mail. Sometimes, the threat of substitution is downstream or indirect, when a substitute replaces a buyer industry's product. For example, lawn-care products and services are threatened when multifamily homes in urban areas substitute for single-family homes in the suburbs. Software sold to agents is threatened when airline and travel websites substitute for travel agents.

Substitutes are always present, but they are easy to overlook because they may appear to be very different from the industry's product: To someone searching for a Father's Day gift, neckties and power tools may be substitutes. It is a substitute to do without, to purchase a used product rather than a new one, or to do it yourself (bring the service or product in-house).

When the threat of substitutes is high, industry profitability suffers. Substitute products or services limit an industry's profit potential by placing a ceiling on prices. If an industry does not distance itself from substitutes through product performance, marketing, or other means, it will suffer in terms of profitability—and often growth potential.

Substitutes not only limit profits in normal times but also reduce the bonanza an industry can reap in good times. In emerging economies, for example, the surge in demand for wired telephone lines has been capped as many consumers opt to make a mobile telephone their first and only phone line.

The threat of a substitute is high if:

- It offers an attractive price-performance trade-off to the industry's product. The better the relative value of the substitute, the tighter the lid on an industry's profit potential. For example, conventional providers of long-distance telephone service have suffered from the advent of inexpensive internet-based phone services such as Vonage and Skype. Similarly, video rental outlets are struggling with the emergence of cable and satellite video-on-demand services, online video rental services such as Netflix, and the rise of internet video sites like Google's YouTube.

- The buyer's cost of switching to the substitute is low. Switching from a proprietary, branded drug to a generic drug usually involves minimal costs, for example, which is why the shift to generics (and the fall in prices) is so substantial and rapid.

Strategists should be particularly alert to changes in other industries that may make them attractive substitutes when they were not before. Improvements in plastic materials, for example, allowed them to substitute for steel in many automobile components. In this way, technological changes or competitive discontinuities in seemingly unrelated businesses can have major impacts on industry profitability. Of course, the substitution threat can also shift in favor of an industry, which bodes well for its future profitability and growth potential.

Rivalry among existing competitors

Rivalry among existing competitors takes many familiar forms, including price discounting, new product introductions, advertising campaigns, and service improvements. High rivalry limits the profitability of an industry. The degree to which rivalry drives down an industry's profit potential depends, first, on the *intensity* with which companies compete and, second, on the *basis* on which they compete.

The intensity of rivalry is greatest if:

- Competitors are numerous or are roughly equal in size and power. In such situations, rivals find it hard to avoid poaching business. Without an industry leader, practices desirable for the industry as a whole go unenforced.

- Industry growth is slow. Slow growth precipitates fights for market share.

- Exit barriers are high. Exit barriers, the flip side of entry barriers, arise because of such things as highly specialized assets or management's devotion to a particular business. These barriers keep companies in the market even though they may be earning low or negative returns. Excess capacity remains in use, and the profitability of healthy competitors suffers as the sick ones hang on.

- Rivals are highly committed to the business and have aspirations for leadership, especially if they have goals that go beyond economic performance in the particular industry. High commitment to a business arises for a variety of reasons. For example, state-owned competitors may have goals that include employment or prestige. Units of larger companies may participate in an industry for image reasons or to offer a full line. Clashes of personality and ego have sometimes exaggerated rivalry to the detriment of profitability in fields such as the media and high technology.

- Firms cannot read each other's signals well because of lack of familiarity with one another, diverse approaches to competing, or differing goals.

The strength of rivalry reflects not just the intensity of competition but also the basis of competition. The *dimensions* on which competition takes place and whether rivals converge to compete on the *same dimensions* have a major influence on profitability.

Rivalry is especially destructive to profitability if it gravitates solely to price because price competition transfers profits directly from an industry to its customers. Price cuts are usually easy for competitors to see and match, making successive rounds of retaliation likely. Sustained price competition also trains customers to pay less attention to product features and service.

Price competition is most liable to occur if:

- Products or services of rivals are nearly identical and there are few switching costs for buyers. This encourages competitors to cut prices to win new customers. Years of airline price wars reflect these circumstances in that industry.

- Fixed costs are high and marginal costs are low. This creates intense pressure for competitors to cut prices below their average costs, even close to their marginal costs, to steal incremental customers while still making some contribution to covering fixed costs. Many basic-materials businesses, such as paper and aluminum, suffer from this problem, especially if demand is not growing. The case is the same for delivery companies with fixed networks of routes that must be served regardless of volume.

- Capacity must be expanded in large increments to be efficient. The need for large capacity expansions, as in the polyvinyl chloride business, disrupts the industry's supply-demand balance and often leads to long and recurring periods of overcapacity and price cutting.

- The product is perishable. Perishability creates a strong temptation to cut prices and sell a product while it still has value. More products and services are perishable than is commonly thought. Just as tomatoes are perishable because they rot, models of computers are perishable because they soon become obsolete, and information may be perishable if it diffuses rapidly or becomes outdated, thereby losing its value. Services such as hotel accommodations are perishable in the sense that unused capacity can never be recovered.

Competition on dimensions other than price—on product features, support services, delivery time, or brand image, for instance—is less likely to erode profitability because it improves customer value and can support higher prices. Also, rivalry focused on such dimensions can improve value relative to substitutes or raise the barriers facing new entrants. While nonprice rivalry sometimes escalates to levels that undermine industry profitability, this is less likely to occur than it is with price rivalry.

As important as the dimensions of rivalry is whether rivals compete on the *same* dimensions. When all or many competitors aim to meet the same needs or compete on the same attributes, the result is zero-sum competition. Here, one firm's gain is often another's loss, driving down profitability. While price competition runs a stronger risk than nonprice competition of becoming zero sum, this may not happen if companies take care to segment their markets, targeting their low-price offerings to different customers.

Rivalry can be positive sum, or actually increase the average profitability of an industry, when each competitor aims to serve the needs of different customer segments, with different mixes of price, products, services, features, or brand identities. Such competition can not only support higher average profitability but also expand the industry, as the needs of more customer groups are better met. The opportunity for positive-sum competition will be greater in industries serving diverse customer groups. With a clear understanding of the structural underpinnings of rivalry, strategists can sometimes take steps to shift the nature of competition in a more positive direction.

Factors, Not Forces

Industry structure, as manifested in the strength of the five competitive forces, determines the industry's long-run profit potential because it determines how the economic value created by the industry is divided—how much is retained by companies in the industry versus bargained away by customers and suppliers, limited by substitutes, or constrained by potential new entrants. By considering all five forces, a strategist keeps overall structure in mind instead of gravitating to any one element. In addition, the strategist's attention remains focused on structural conditions rather than on fleeting factors.

It is especially important to avoid the common pitfall of mistaking certain visible attributes of an industry for its underlying structure. Consider the following:

Industry growth rate

A common mistake is to assume that fast-growing industries are always attractive. Growth does tend to mute rivalry, because an expanding pie offers opportunities for all competitors. But fast growth can put suppliers in a powerful position, and high growth with low entry barriers will draw in entrants. Even without new entrants, a high growth rate will not guarantee profitability if customers are powerful or substitutes are attractive. Indeed, some fast-growth businesses, such as personal computers, have been among the least profitable industries in recent years. A narrow focus on growth is one of the major causes of bad strategy decisions.

Technology and innovation

Advanced technology or innovations are not by themselves enough to make an industry structurally attractive (or unattractive). Mundane, low-technology industries with price-insensitive buyers, high switching costs, or high entry barriers arising from scale economies are often far more profitable than sexy industries, such as software and internet technologies, that attract competitors.

Government

Government is not best understood as a sixth force because government involvement is neither inherently good nor bad for industry profitability. The best way to understand the influence of government on competition is to analyze how specific government policies affect the five competitive forces. For instance, patents raise barriers to entry, boosting industry profit potential. Conversely, government policies favoring unions may raise supplier power and diminish profit potential. Bankruptcy rules that allow failing companies to reorganize rather than exit can lead to excess capacity and intense rivalry. Government operates at multiple levels and through many different policies, each of which will affect structure in different ways.

Complementary products and services

Complements are products or services used together with an industry's product. Complements arise when the customer benefit of two products combined is greater than the sum of each product's value in isolation. Computer hardware and software, for instance, are valuable together and worthless when separated.

In recent years, strategy researchers have highlighted the role of complements, especially in high-technology industries where they are most obvious. By no means, however, do complements appear only there. The value of a car, for example, is greater when the driver also has access to gasoline stations, roadside assistance, and auto insurance.

Complements can be important when they affect the overall demand for an industry's product. However, like government policy, complements are not a sixth force determining industry profitability since the presence of strong complements is not necessarily bad (or good) for industry profitability. Complements affect profitability through the way they influence the five forces.

The strategist must trace the positive or negative influence of complements on all five forces to ascertain their impact on profitability. The presence of complements can raise or lower barriers to entry. In application software, for example, barriers to entry were lowered when producers of complementary operating system software, notably Microsoft, provided tool sets making it easier to write applications. Conversely, the need to attract producers of complements can raise barriers to entry, as it does in video game hardware.

The presence of complements can also affect the threat of substitutes. For instance, the need for appropriate fueling stations makes it difficult for cars using alternative fuels to substitute for conventional vehicles. But complements can also make substitution easier. For example, Apple's iTunes hastened the substitution from CDs to digital music.

Complements can factor into industry rivalry either positively (as when they raise switching costs) or negatively (as when they neutralize product differentiation). Similar analyses can be done for buyer and supplier power. Sometimes companies compete by altering conditions in complementary industries in their favor, such as when videocassette-recorder producer JVC persuaded movie studios to favor its standard in issuing prerecorded tapes even though rival Sony's standard was probably superior from a technical standpoint.

Identifying complements is part of the analyst's work. As with government policies or important technologies, the strategic significance of complements will be best understood through the lens of the five forces.

Changes in Industry Structure

So far, we have discussed the competitive forces at a single point in time. Industry structure proves to be relatively stable, and industry profitability differences are remarkably persistent over time in practice. However, industry structure is constantly undergoing modest adjustment—and occasionally it can change abruptly.

Shifts in structure may emanate from outside an industry or from within. They can boost the industry's profit potential or reduce it. They may be caused by changes in technology, changes in customer needs, or other events. The five competitive forces provide a framework for identifying the most important industry developments and for anticipating their impact on industry attractiveness.

Shifting threat of new entry

Changes to any of the seven barriers described above can raise or lower the threat of new entry. The expiration of a patent, for instance, may unleash new entrants. On the day that Merck's patents for the cholesterol reducer Zocor expired, three pharmaceutical makers entered the market for the drug. Conversely, the proliferation of products in the ice cream industry has gradually filled up the limited freezer space in grocery stores, making it harder for new ice cream makers to gain access to distribution in North America and Europe.

Strategic decisions of leading competitors often have a major impact on the threat of entry. Starting in the 1970s, for example, retailers such as Walmart, Kmart, and Toys "R" Us began to adopt new procurement, distribution, and inventory control technologies with large fixed costs, including automated distribution centers, bar coding, and point-of-sale terminals. These investments increased the economies of scale and made it more difficult for small retailers to enter the business (and for existing small players to survive).

Changing supplier or buyer power

As the factors underlying the power of suppliers and buyers change with time, their clout rises or declines. In the global appliance industry, for instance, competitors including Electrolux, General Electric, and Whirlpool have been squeezed by the consolidation of retail channels (the decline of appliance specialty stores, for instance, and the rise of big-box retailers like Best Buy and Home Depot in the United States). Another example is travel agents, who depend on airlines as a key supplier. When the internet allowed airlines to sell tickets directly to customers, this significantly increased their power to bargain down agents' commissions.

Shifting threat of substitution

The most common reason substitutes become more or less threatening over time is that advances in technology create new substitutes or shift price-performance comparisons in one direction or the other. The earliest microwave ovens, for example, were large and priced above $2,000, making them poor substitutes for conventional ovens. With technological advances, they became serious substitutes. Flash computer memory has improved enough recently to become a meaningful substitute for low-capacity hard-disk drives. Trends in the availability or performance of complementary producers also shift the threat of substitutes.

New bases of rivalry

Rivalry often intensifies naturally over time. As an industry matures, growth slows. Competitors become more alike as industry conventions emerge, technology diffuses, and consumer tastes converge. Industry profitability falls, and weaker competitors are driven from the business. This story has played out in industry after industry; televisions, snowmobiles, and telecommunications equipment are just a few examples.

A trend toward intensifying price competition and other forms of rivalry, however, is by no means inevitable. For example, there has been enormous competitive activity in the U.S. casino industry in recent decades, but most of it has been positive-sum competition directed toward new niches and geographic segments (such as riverboats, trophy properties, Native American reservations, international expansion, and novel customer groups like families). Head-to-head rivalry that lowers prices or boosts the payouts to winners has been limited.

The nature of rivalry in an industry is altered by mergers and acquisitions that introduce new capabilities and ways of competing. Or technological innovation can reshape rivalry. In the retail brokerage industry, the advent of the internet lowered marginal costs and reduced differentiation, triggering far more intense competition on commissions and fees than in the past.

In some industries, companies turn to mergers and consolidation not to improve cost and quality but to attempt to stop intense competition. Eliminating rivals is a risky strategy, however. The five competitive forces tell us that a profit windfall from removing today's competitors often attracts new competitors and backlash from customers and suppliers. In New York banking, for example, the 1980s and 1990s saw escalating consolidations of commercial and savings banks, including Manufacturers Hanover, Chemical, Chase, and Dime Savings. But today the retail-banking landscape of Manhattan is as diverse as ever, as new entrants such as Wachovia, Bank of America, and Washington Mutual have entered the market.

Implications for Strategy

Understanding the forces that shape industry competition is the starting point for developing strategy. Every company should already know what the average profitability of its industry is and how that has been changing over time. The five forces reveal *why* industry profitability is what it is. Only then can a company incorporate industry conditions into strategy.

The forces reveal the most significant aspects of the competitive environment. They also provide a baseline for sizing up a company's strengths and weaknesses: Where does the company stand versus buyers, suppliers, entrants, rivals, and substitutes? Most importantly, an understanding of industry structure guides managers toward fruitful possibilities for strategic action, which may include any or all of the following: positioning the company to better cope with the current competitive forces; anticipating and exploiting shifts in the forces; and shaping the balance of forces to create a new industry structure that is more favorable to the company. The best strategies exploit more than one of these possibilities.

Positioning the company

Strategy can be viewed as building defenses against the competitive forces or finding a position in the industry where the forces are weakest. Consider, for instance, the position of Paccar in the market for heavy trucks. The heavy-truck industry is structurally challenging. Many buyers operate large fleets or are large leasing companies, with both the leverage and the motivation to drive down the price of one of their largest purchases. Most trucks are built to regulated standards and offer similar features, so price competition is rampant. Capital intensity causes rivalry to be fierce, especially during the recurring cyclical downturns. Unions exercise considerable supplier power. Though there are few direct substitutes for an 18-wheeler, truck buyers face important substitutes for their services, such as cargo delivery by rail.

In this setting, Paccar, a Bellevue, Washington–based company with about 20% of the North American heavy-truck market, has chosen to focus on one group of customers: owner-operators— drivers who own their trucks and contract directly with shippers or serve as subcontractors to larger trucking companies. Such small operators have limited clout as truck buyers. They are also less price sensitive because of their strong emotional ties to and economic dependence on the product. They take great pride in their trucks, in which they spend most of their time.

Paccar has invested heavily to develop an array of features with owner-operators in mind: luxurious sleeper cabins, plush leather seats, noise-insulated cabins, sleek exterior styling, and so on. At the company's extensive network of dealers, prospective buyers use software to select among thousands of options to put their personal signature on their trucks. These customized trucks are built to order, not to stock, and delivered in six to eight weeks. Paccar's trucks also have aerodynamic designs that reduce fuel consumption, and they maintain their resale value better than other trucks. Paccar's roadside assistance program and IT-supported system for distributing spare parts reduce the time a truck is out of service. All these are crucial considerations for an owner-operator. Customers pay Paccar a 10% premium, and its Kenworth and Peterbilt brands are considered status symbols at truck stops.

Paccar illustrates the principles of positioning a company within a given industry structure. The firm has found a portion of its industry where the competitive forces are weaker—where it can avoid buyer power and price-based rivalry. And it has tailored every single part of the value chain to cope well with the forces in its segment. As a result, Paccar has been profitable for 68 years straight and has earned a long-run return on equity above 20%.

In addition to revealing positioning opportunities within an existing industry, the five forces framework allows companies to rigorously analyze entry and exit. Both depend on answering the difficult question: "What is the potential of this business?"

Exit is indicated when industry structure is poor or declining and the company has no prospect of a superior positioning. In considering entry into a new industry, creative strategists can use the framework to spot an industry with a good future before this good future is reflected in the prices of acquisition candidates. Five forces analysis may also reveal industries that are not necessarily attractive for the average entrant but in which a company has good reason to believe it can surmount entry barriers at lower cost than most firms or has a unique ability to cope with the industry's competitive forces.

Exploiting industry change

Industry changes bring the opportunity to spot and claim promising new strategic positions if the strategist has a sophisticated understanding of the competitive forces and their underpinnings. Consider, for instance, the evolution of the music industry during the past decade. With the advent of the internet and the digital distribution of music, some analysts predicted the birth of thousands of music labels (that is, record companies that develop artists and bring their music to market). This, the analysts argued, would break a pattern that had held since Edison invented the phonograph: Between three and six major record companies had always dominated the industry. The internet would, they predicted, remove distribution as a barrier to entry, unleashing a flood of new players into the music industry.

A careful analysis, however, would have revealed that physical distribution was not the crucial barrier to entry. Rather, entry was barred by other benefits that large music labels enjoyed. Large labels could pool the risks of developing new artists over many bets, cushioning the impact of inevitable failures. Even more important, they had advantages in breaking through the clutter and getting their new artists heard. To do so, they could promise radio stations and record stores access to well-known artists in exchange for promotion of new artists. New labels would find this nearly impossible to match. The major labels stayed the course, and new music labels have been rare.

This is not to say that the music industry is structurally un-changed by digital distribution. Unauthorized downloading cre-ated an illegal but potent substitute. The labels tried for years to develop technical platforms for digital distribution themselves, but major companies hesitated to sell their music through a plat-form owned by a rival. Into this vacuum stepped Apple with its iTunes music store, launched in 2003 to support its iPod music player. By permitting the creation of a powerful new gatekeeper, the major labels allowed industry structure to shift against them. The number of major record companies has actually declined—from six in 1997 to four today—as companies struggled to cope with the digital phenomenon.

When industry structure is in flux, new and promising com-petitive positions may appear. Structural changes open up new needs and new ways to serve existing needs. Established leaders may overlook these or be constrained by past strategies from pur-suing them. Smaller competitors in the industry can capitalize on such changes, or the void may well be filled by new entrants.

Shaping industry structure

When a company exploits structural change, it is recognizing, and reacting to, the inevitable. However, companies also have the ability to shape industry structure. A firm can lead its indus-try toward new ways of competing that alter the five forces for the better. In reshaping structure, a company wants its competitors to follow so that the entire industry will be transformed. While many industry participants may benefit in the process, the innovator can benefit most if it can shift competition in directions where it can excel.

An industry's structure can be reshaped in two ways: by redividing profitability in favor of incumbents or by expanding the overall profit pool. Redividing the industry pie aims to increase the share of profits to industry competitors instead of to suppliers, buyers, substitutes, and keeping out potential entrants. Expanding the profit pool involves increasing the overall pool of economic value generated by the industry in which rivals, buyers, and suppliers can all share.

Redividing profitability. To capture more profits for industry rivals, the starting point is to determine which force or forces are currently constraining industry profitability and address them. A company can potentially influence all of the competitive forces. The strategist's goal here is to reduce the share of profits that leak to suppliers, buyers, and substitutes or are sacrificed to deter entrants.

To neutralize supplier power, for example, a firm can standardize specifications for parts to make it easier to switch among suppliers. It can cultivate additional vendors, or alter technology to avoid a powerful supplier group altogether. To counter customer power, companies may expand services that raise buyers' switching costs or find alternative means of reaching customers to neutralize powerful channels. To temper profit-eroding price rivalry, companies can invest more heavily in unique products, as pharmaceutical firms have done, or expand support services to customers. To scare off entrants, incumbents can elevate the fixed cost of competing—for instance, by escalating their R&D or marketing expenditures. To limit the threat of substitutes, companies can offer better value through new features or wider product accessibility. When soft-drink producers introduced vending machines and convenience store channels, for example, they dramatically improved the availability of soft drinks relative to other beverages.

Sysco, the largest food-service distributor in North America, offers a revealing example of how an industry leader can change the structure of an industry for the better. Food-service distributors purchase food and related items from farmers and food processors. They then warehouse and deliver these items to restaurants, hospitals, employer cafeterias, schools, and other food-service institutions. Given low barriers to entry, the food-service distribution industry has historically been highly fragmented, with numerous local competitors. While rivals try to cultivate customer relationships, buyers are price sensitive because food represents a large share of their costs. Buyers can also choose the substitute approaches of purchasing directly from manufacturers or using retail sources, avoiding distributors altogether. Suppliers wield bargaining power: They are often large companies with strong brand names that food preparers and consumers recognize. Average profitability in the industry has been modest.

Sysco recognized that, given its size and national reach, it might change this state of affairs. It led the move to introduce private-label distributor brands with specifications tailored to the food-service market, moderating supplier power. Sysco emphasized value-added services to buyers such as credit, menu planning, and inventory management to shift the basis of competition away from just price. These moves, together with stepped-up investments in information technology and regional distribution centers, substantially raised the bar for new entrants while making the substitutes less attractive. Not surprisingly, the industry has been consolidating, and industry profitability appears to be rising.

Industry leaders have a special responsibility for improving industry structure. Doing so often requires resources that only large players possess. Moreover, an improved industry structure is a public good because it benefits every firm in the industry, not just the company that initiated the improvement. Often, it is more in the interests of an industry leader than any other participant to invest for the common good because leaders will usually benefit the most. Indeed, improving the industry may be a leader's most profitable strategic opportunity, in part because attempts to gain further market share can trigger strong reactions from rivals, customers, and even suppliers.

There is a dark side to shaping industry structure that is equally important to understand. Ill-advised changes in competitive positioning and operating practices can *undermine* industry structure. Faced with pressures to gain market share or enamored with innovation for its own sake, managers may trigger new kinds of competition that no incumbent can win. When taking actions to improve their own company's competitive advantage, then, strategists should ask whether they are setting in motion dynamics that will undermine industry structure in the long run. In the early days of the personal computer industry, for instance, IBM tried to make up for its late entry by offering an open architecture that would set industry standards and attract complementary makers of application software and peripherals. In the process, it ceded ownership of the critical components of the PC—the operating system and the microprocessor—to Microsoft and Intel. By standardizing PCs, it encouraged price-based rivalry and shifted power to suppliers. Consequently, IBM became the temporarily dominant firm in an industry with an enduringly unattractive structure.

Expanding the profit pool. When overall demand grows, the industry's quality level rises, intrinsic costs are reduced, or waste is eliminated, the pie expands. The total pool of value available to competitors, suppliers, and buyers grows. The total profit pool expands, for example, when channels become more competitive or when an industry discovers latent buyers for its product that are not currently being served. When soft-drink producers rationalized their independent bottler networks to make them more efficient and effective, both the soft-drink companies and the bottlers benefited. Overall value can also expand when firms work collaboratively with suppliers to improve coordination and limit unnecessary costs incurred in the supply chain. This lowers the inherent cost structure of the industry, allowing higher profit, greater demand through lower prices, or both. Or agreeing on quality standards can bring up industrywide quality and service levels and hence prices, benefiting rivals, suppliers, and customers.

Expanding the overall profit pool creates win-win opportunities for multiple industry participants. It can also reduce the risk of destructive rivalry that arises when incumbents attempt to shift bargaining power or capture more market share. However, expanding the pie does not reduce the importance of industry structure. How the expanded pie is divided will ultimately be determined by the five forces. The most successful companies are those that expand the industry profit pool in ways that allow them to share disproportionately in the benefits.

Defining the industry

The five competitive forces also hold the key to defining the relevant industry (or industries) in which a company competes. Drawing industry boundaries correctly, around the arena in

Defining the Relevant Industry

Defining the industry in which competition actually takes place is important for good industry analysis, not to mention for developing strategy and setting business unit boundaries. Many strategy errors emanate from mistaking the relevant industry, defining it too broadly or too narrowly. Defining the industry too broadly obscures differences among products, customers, or geographic regions that are important to competition, strategic positioning, and profitability. Defining the industry too narrowly overlooks commonalities and linkages across related products or geographic markets that are crucial to competitive advantage. Also, strategists must be sensitive to the possibility that industry boundaries can shift.

The boundaries of an industry consist of two primary dimensions. First is the *scope of products or services*. For example, is motor oil used in cars part of the same industry as motor oil used in heavy trucks and stationary engines, or are these different industries? The second dimension is *geographic scope*. Most industries are present in many parts of the world. However, is competition contained within each state, or is it national? Does competition take place within regions such as Europe or North America, or is there a single global industry?

The five forces are the basic tool to resolve these questions. If industry structure for two products is the same or very similar (that is, if they have the same buyers, suppliers, barriers to entry, and so forth), then the products are best treated as being part of the same industry. If industry structure differs markedly, however, the two products may be best understood as separate industries.

In lubricants, the oil used in cars is similar or even identical to the oil used in trucks, but the similarity largely ends there. Automotive motor oil is sold to fragmented, generally unsophisticated customers through numerous and often powerful channels, using extensive advertising. Products are packaged in small containers and logistical costs are high, necessitating local production. Truck and power generation lubricants are sold to entirely different buyers in entirely different ways using a separate supply

(continued)

Defining the Relevant Industry (*continued*)

chain. Industry structure (buyer power, barriers to entry, and so forth) is substantially different. Automotive oil is thus a distinct industry from oil for truck and stationary engine uses. Industry profitability will differ in these two cases, and a lubricant company will need a separate strategy for competing in each area.

Differences in the five competitive forces also reveal the geographic scope of competition. If an industry has a similar structure in every country (rivals, buyers, and so on), the presumption is that competition is global, and the five forces analyzed from a global perspective will set average profitability. A single global strategy is needed. If an industry has quite different structures in different geographic regions, however, each region may well be a distinct industry. Otherwise, competition would have leveled the differences. The five forces analyzed for each region will set profitability there.

The extent of differences in the five forces for related products or across geographic areas is a matter of degree, making industry definition often a matter of judgment. A rule of thumb is that where the differences in any one force are large, and where the differences involve more than one force, distinct industries may well be present.

Fortunately, however, even if industry boundaries are drawn incorrectly, careful five forces analysis should reveal important competitive threats. A closely related product omitted from the industry definition will show up as a substitute, for example, or competitors overlooked as rivals will be recognized as potential entrants. At the same time, the five forces analysis should reveal major differences within overly broad industries that will indicate the need to adjust industry boundaries or strategies.

which competition actually takes place, will clarify the causes of profitability and the appropriate unit for setting strategy. A company needs a separate strategy for each distinct industry. Mistakes in industry definition made by competitors present opportunities for staking out superior strategic positions. (See the sidebar "Defining the Relevant Industry.")

Competition and Value

The competitive forces reveal the drivers of industry competition. A company strategist who understands that competition extends well beyond existing rivals will detect wider competitive threats and be better equipped to address them. At the same time, thinking comprehensively about an industry's structure can uncover opportunities: differences in customers, suppliers, substitutes, potential entrants, and rivals that can become the basis for distinct strategies yielding superior performance. In a world of more open competition and relentless change, it is more important than ever to think structurally about competition.

Understanding industry structure is equally important for investors as for managers. The five competitive forces reveal whether an industry is truly attractive, and they help investors anticipate positive or negative shifts in industry structure before they are obvious. The five forces distinguish short-term blips from structural changes and allow investors to take advantage of undue pessimism or optimism. Those companies whose strategies have industry-transforming potential become far clearer. This deeper thinking about competition is a more powerful way to achieve genuine investment success than the financial projections and trend extrapolation that dominate today's investment analysis.

Typical Steps in Industry Analysis

Define the relevant industry:

- What products are in it? Which ones are part of another distinct industry?

- What is the geographic scope of competition?

Identify the participants and segment them into groups, if appropriate. Who are:

- the buyers and buyer groups?

- the suppliers and supplier groups?

- the competitors?

- the substitutes?

- the potential entrants?

Assess the underlying drivers of each competitive force to determine which forces are strong and which are weak and why.

Determine overall industry structure, and test the analysis for consistency:

- *Why* is the level of profitability what it is?

- Which are the *controlling* forces for profitability?

- Is the industry analysis consistent with actual long-run profitability?

- Are more-profitable players better positioned in relation to the five forces?

Analyze recent and likely future changes in each force, both positive and negative.

Identify aspects of industry structure that might be influenced by competitors, by new entrants, or by your company.

Common Pitfalls

In conducting the analysis, avoid the following common mistakes:

- Defining the industry too broadly or too narrowly.

- Making lists instead of engaging in rigorous analysis.

- Paying equal attention to all of the forces rather than digging deeply into the most important ones.

- Confusing effect (price sensitivity) with cause (buyer economics).

- Using static analysis that ignores industry trends.

- Confusing cyclical or transient changes with true structural changes.

- Using the framework to declare an industry attractive or unattractive rather than using it to guide strategic choices.

If both executives and investors looked at competition this way, capital markets would be a far more effective force for company success and economic prosperity. Executives and investors would both be focused on the same fundamentals that drive sustained profitability. The conversation between investors and executives would focus on the structural, not the transient. Imagine the improvement in company performance—and in the economy as a whole—if all the energy expended in "pleasing the Street" were redirected toward the factors that create true economic value.

Originally published in May 2011. Reprint R0801E

2

Blue Ocean Strategy

by W. Chan Kim and Renée Mauborgne

A onetime accordion player, stilt walker, and fire-eater, Guy Laliberté is now CEO of one of Canada's largest cultural exports, Cirque du Soleil. Founded in 1984 by a group of street performers, Cirque has staged dozens of productions seen by some 40 million people in 90 cities around the world. In 20 years, Cirque has achieved revenues that Ringling Bros. and Barnum & Bailey—the world's leading circus—took more than a century to attain.

Cirque's rapid growth occurred in an unlikely setting. The circus business was (and still is) in long-term decline. Alternative forms of entertainment—sporting events, TV, and video games—were casting a growing shadow. Children, the mainstay of the circus audience, preferred PlayStations to circus acts. There was also rising sentiment, fueled by animal rights groups, against the use of animals, traditionally an integral part of the circus. On the supply side, the star performers that Ringling and the other circuses relied on to draw in the crowds could often name their own terms. As a result, the industry was hit by steadily decreasing audiences and increasing costs. What's more, any new entrant to this business would be competing against a formidable incumbent that for most of the last century had set the industry standard.

How did Cirque profitably increase revenues by a factor of 22 over the last 10 years in such an unattractive environment? The tagline for one of the first Cirque productions is revealing: "We reinvent the circus." Cirque did not make its money by competing within the confines of the existing industry or by stealing customers from Ringling and the others. Instead it created uncontested market space that made the competition irrelevant. It pulled in a whole new group of customers who were traditionally noncustomers of the industry—adults and corporate clients who had turned to theater, opera, or ballet and were, therefore, prepared to pay several times more than the price of a conventional circus ticket for an unprecedented entertainment experience.

To understand the nature of Cirque's achievement, you have to realize that the business universe consists of two distinct kinds of space, which we think of as red and blue oceans. Red oceans represent all the industries in existence today—the known market space. In red oceans, industry boundaries are defined and accepted, and the competitive rules of the game are well understood. Here, companies try to outperform their rivals in order to grab a greater share of existing demand. As the space gets more and more crowded, prospects for profits and growth are reduced. Products turn into commodities, and increasing competition turns the water bloody.

Blue oceans denote all the industries *not* in existence today—the unknown market space, untainted by competition. In blue oceans, demand is created rather than fought over. There is ample opportunity for growth that is both profitable and rapid. There are two ways to create blue oceans. In a few cases, companies can

Idea in Brief

The best way to drive profitable growth? Stop competing in overcrowded industries. In those red oceans, companies try to outperform rivals to grab bigger slices of existing demand. As the space gets increasingly crowded, profit and growth prospects shrink. Products become commoditized. Ever-more-intense competition turns the water bloody.

How to avoid the fray? Kim and Mauborgne recommend creating blue oceans—uncontested market spaces where the competition is irrelevant. In blue oceans, you invent and capture new demand, and you offer customers a leap in value while also streamlining your costs. Results? Handsome profits, speedy growth—and brand equity that lasts for decades while rivals scramble to catch up.

Consider Cirque du Soleil—which invented a new industry that combined elements from traditional circus with elements drawn from sophisticated theater. In just 20 years, Cirque raked in revenues that Ringling Bros. and Barnum & Bailey—the world's leading circus—needed more than a century to attain.

give rise to completely new industries, as eBay did with the online auction industry. But in most cases, a blue ocean is created from within a red ocean when a company alters the boundaries of an existing industry. As will become evident later, this is what Cirque did. In breaking through the boundary traditionally separating circus and theater, it made a new and profitable blue ocean from within the red ocean of the circus industry.

Cirque is just one of more than 150 blue ocean creations that we have studied in over 30 industries, using data stretching back more than 100 years. We analyzed companies that created those blue oceans and their less successful competitors, which were caught in red oceans. In studying this data, we have observed a consistent pattern of strategic thinking behind the creation of new markets and industries, what we call blue ocean strategy. The logic behind blue ocean strategy parts with traditional models focused on competing in existing market space.

Indeed, it can be argued that managers' failure to realize the differences between red and blue ocean strategy lies behind the difficulties many companies encounter as they try to break from the competition.

In this article, we present the concept of blue ocean strategy and describe its defining characteristics. We assess the profit and growth consequences of blue oceans and discuss why their creation is a rising imperative for companies in the future. We believe that an understanding of blue ocean strategy will help today's companies as they struggle to thrive in an accelerating and expanding business universe.

Blue and Red Oceans

Although the term may be new, blue oceans have always been with us. Look back 100 years and ask yourself which industries known today were then unknown. The answer: Industries as basic as automobiles, music recording, aviation, petrochemicals, pharmaceuticals, and management consulting were unheard-of or had just begun to emerge. Now turn the clock back only 30 years and ask yourself the same question. Again, a plethora of multibillion-dollar industries jump out: mutual funds, cellular telephones, biotechnology, discount retailing, express package delivery, snowboards, coffee bars, and home videos, to name a few. Just three decades ago, none of these industries existed in a meaningful way.

This time, put the clock forward 20 years. Ask yourself: How many industries that are unknown today will exist then? If history is any predictor of the future, the answer is many. Companies have a huge capacity to create new industries and re-create existing ones, a fact that is reflected in the deep changes that have been necessary in the way industries are classified. The half-century-old Standard Industrial Classification (SIC) system was replaced in 1997 by the North American Industry Classification System (NAICS). The new system expanded the 10 SIC industry sectors into 20 to reflect the emerging realities of new industry territories—blue oceans. The services sector under the old system, for example, is now seven sectors ranging from information to health care and social assistance. Given that these classification systems are designed for standardization and continuity, such a replacement shows how significant a source of economic growth the creation of blue oceans has been.

Looking forward, it seems clear to us that blue oceans will remain the engine of growth. Prospects in most established market spaces—red oceans—are shrinking steadily. Technological advances have substantially improved industrial productivity, permitting suppliers to produce an unprecedented array of products and services. And as trade barriers between nations and regions fall and information on products and prices becomes instantly and globally available, niche markets and monopoly havens are continuing to disappear. At the same time, there is little evidence of any increase in demand, at least in the developed markets, where recent United Nations statistics even point to declining populations. The result is that in more and more industries, supply is overtaking demand.

This situation has inevitably hastened the commoditization of products and services, stoked price wars, and shrunk profit margins. According to recent studies, major American brands in a variety of product and service categories have become more and more alike. And as brands become more similar, people increasingly base purchase choices on price. People no longer insist, as in the past, that their laundry detergent be Tide. Nor do they necessarily stick to Colgate when there is a special promotion for Crest, and vice versa. In overcrowded industries, differentiating brands becomes harder both in economic upturns and in downturns.

The Paradox of Strategy

Unfortunately, most companies seem becalmed in their red oceans. In a study of business launches in 108 companies, we found that 86% of those new ventures were line extensions—incremental improvements to existing industry offerings—and a mere 14% were aimed at creating new markets or industries. While line extensions did account for 62% of the total revenues, they delivered only 39% of the total profits. By contrast, the 14% invested in creating new markets and industries delivered 38% of total revenues and a startling 61% of total profits.

So why the dramatic imbalance in favor of red oceans? Part of the explanation is that corporate strategy is heavily influenced by its roots in military strategy. The very language of strategy is deeply imbued with military references—chief executive "officers" in "headquarters," "troops" on the "front lines." Described this way, strategy is all about red ocean competition. It is about confronting an opponent and driving him off a battlefield of limited territory. Blue ocean strategy, by contrast, is about doing business where there is no competitor. It is about creating new land, not dividing up existing land. Focusing on the red ocean therefore means accepting the key constraining factors of war—limited terrain and the need to beat an enemy to succeed. And it means denying the distinctive strength of the business world—the capacity to create new market space that is uncontested.

The tendency of corporate strategy to focus on winning against rivals was exacerbated by the meteoric rise of Japanese companies in the 1970s and 1980s. For the first time in corporate history, customers were deserting Western companies in droves. As competition mounted in the global marketplace, a slew of red ocean strategies emerged, all arguing that competition was at the core of corporate success and failure. Today, one hardly talks about strategy without using the language of competition. The term that best symbolizes this is "competitive advantage." In the competitive-advantage worldview, companies are often driven to outperform rivals and capture greater shares of existing market space.

Of course competition matters. But by focusing on competition, scholars, companies, and consultants have ignored two very important—and, we would argue, far more lucrative—aspects of strategy: One is to find and develop markets where there is little or no competition—blue oceans—and the other is to exploit and protect blue oceans. These challenges are very different from those to which strategists have devoted most of their attention.

Toward Blue Ocean Strategy

What kind of strategic logic is needed to guide the creation of blue oceans? To answer that question, we looked back over 100 years of data on blue ocean creation to see what patterns could be discerned. Some of our data are presented in the exhibit "A snapshot of blue ocean creation." It shows an overview of key blue ocean creations in three industries that closely touch people's lives: autos—how people get to work; computers—what people use at work; and movie theaters—where people go after work for enjoyment.

A snapshot of blue ocean creation

This table identifies the strategic elements that were common to blue ocean creations in three different industries in different eras. It is not intended to be comprehensive in coverage or exhaustive in content. We chose to show American industries because they represented the largest and least-regulated market during our study period. The pattern of blue ocean creations exemplified by these three industries is consistent with what we observed in the other industries in our study.

Key blue ocean creations	Was the blue ocean created by a new entrant or an incumbent?	Was it driven by technology pioneering or value pioneering?	At the time of the blue ocean creation, was the industry attractive or unattractive?
AUTOMOBILES			
Ford Model T Unveiled in 1908, the Model T was the first mass-produced car, priced so that many Americans could afford it.	New entrant	Value pioneering* (mostly existing technologies)	Unattractive
GM's "car for every purse and purpose" GM created a blue ocean in 1924 by injecting fun and fashion into the car.	Incumbent	Value pioneering (some new technologies)	Attractive
Japanese fuel-efficient autos Japanese automakers created a blue ocean in the mid-1970s with small, reliable lines of cars.	Incumbent	Value pioneering (some new technologies)	Unattractive

Chrysler minivan With its 1984 minivan, Chrysler created a new class of automobile that was as easy to use as a car but had the passenger space of a van.	Incumbent	Value pioneering (mostly existing technologies)	Unattractive
COMPUTERS			
CTR's tabulating machine In 1914, CTR created the business machine industry by simplifying, modularizing, and leasing tabulating machines. CTR later changed its name to IBM.	Incumbent	Value pioneering (some new technologies)	Unattractive
IBM 650 electronic computer and System/360 In 1952, IBM created the business computer industry by simplifying and reducing the power and price of existing technology. And it exploded the blue ocean created by the 650 when in 1964 it unveiled the System/360, the first modularized computer system.	Incumbent	Value pioneering (650: mostly existing technologies) Value and technology pioneering (System/360: new and existing technologies)	Nonexistent

(continued)

A snapshot of blue ocean creation (continued)

Key blue ocean creations	Was the blue ocean created by a new entrant or an incumbent?	Was it driven by technology pioneering or value pioneering?	At the time of the blue ocean creation, was the industry attractive or unattractive?
Apple personal computer Although it was not the first home computer, the all-in-one, simple-to-use Apple II was a blue ocean creation when it appeared in 1978.	New entrant	Value pioneering (mostly existing technologies)	Unattractive
Compaq PC servers Compaq created a blue ocean in 1992 with its ProSignia server, which gave buyers twice the file and print capability of the minicomputer at one-third the price.	Incumbent	Value pioneering (mostly existing technologies)	Nonexistent
Dell built-to-order computers In the mid-1990s, Dell created a blue ocean in a highly competitive industry by creating a new purchase and delivery experience for buyers.	New entrant	Value pioneering (mostly existing technologies)	Unattractive
Nickelodeon The first Nickelodeon opened its doors in 1905, showing short films around-the-clock to working-class audiences for five cents.	New entrant	Value pioneering (mostly existing technologies)	Nonexistent

Palace theaters Created by Roxy Rothapfel in 1914, these theaters provided an operalike environment for cinema viewing at an affordable price.	Incumbent	Value pioneering (mostly existing technologies)	Unattractive
AMC multiplex In the 1960s, the number of multiplexes in America's suburban shopping malls mushroomed. The multiplex gave viewers greater choice while reducing owners' costs.	Incumbent	Value pioneering (mostly existing technologies)	Unattractive
AMC megaplex Megaplexes, introduced in 1995, offered every current blockbuster and provided spectacular viewing experiences in theater complexes as big as stadiums, at a lower cost to theater owners.	Incumbent	Value pioneering (mostly existing technologies)	Unattractive

*Driven by value pioneering does not mean that technologies were not involved. Rather, it means that the defining technologies used had largely been in existence, whether in that industry or elsewhere.

We found that:

Blue oceans are not about technology innovation

Leading-edge technology is sometimes involved in the creation of blue oceans, but it is not a defining feature of them. This is often true even in industries that are technology intensive. As the exhibit reveals, across all three representative industries, blue oceans were seldom the result of technological innovation per se; the underlying technology was often already in existence. Even Ford's revolutionary assembly line can be traced to the meatpacking industry in America. Like those within the auto industry, the blue oceans within the computer industry did not come about through technology innovations alone but by linking technology to what buyers valued. As with the IBM 650 and the Compaq PC server, this often involved simplifying the technology.

Incumbents often create blue oceans—and usually within their core businesses

GM, the Japanese automakers, and Chrysler were established players when they created blue oceans in the auto industry. So were CTR and its later incarnation, IBM, and Compaq in the computer industry. And in the cinema industry, the same can be said of palace theaters and AMC. Of the companies listed here, only Ford, Apple, Dell, and Nickelodeon were new entrants in their industries; the first three were startups, and the fourth was an established player entering an industry that was new to it. This suggests that incumbents are not at a disadvantage in creating new market spaces. Moreover, the blue oceans made by incumbents were usually within their core businesses. In fact, as the exhibit shows, most blue oceans are created from within, not beyond, red oceans of existing industries. This challenges the view that new markets are in distant waters. Blue oceans are right next to you in every industry.

Company and industry are the wrong units of analysis

The traditional units of strategic analysis—company and industry—have little explanatory power when it comes to analyzing how and why blue oceans are created. There is no consistently excellent company; the same company can be brilliant at one time and wrongheaded at another. Every company rises and falls over time. Likewise, there is no perpetually excellent industry; relative attractiveness is driven largely by the creation of blue oceans from within them.

The most appropriate unit of analysis for explaining the creation of blue oceans is the strategic move—the set of managerial actions and decisions involved in making a major market-creating business offering. Compaq, for example, is considered by many people to be "unsuccessful" because it was acquired by Hewlett-Packard in 2001 and ceased to be a company. But the firm's ultimate fate does not invalidate the smart strategic move Compaq made that led to the creation of the multibillion-dollar market in PC servers, a move that was a key cause of the company's powerful comeback in the 1990s.

Creating blue oceans builds brands

So powerful is blue ocean strategy that a blue ocean strategic move can create brand equity that lasts for decades. Almost all of the companies listed in the exhibit are remembered in no small part for the blue oceans they created long ago. Very few people alive today were around when the first Model T rolled off Henry Ford's assembly line in 1908, but the company's brand still benefits from that blue ocean move. IBM, too, is often regarded as an American institution largely for the blue oceans it created in computing; the 360 series was its equivalent of the Model T.

Our findings are encouraging for executives at the large, established corporations that are traditionally seen as the victims of new market space creation. For what they reveal is that large R&D budgets are not the key to creating new market space. The key is making the right strategic moves. What's more, companies that understand what drives a good strategic move will be well-placed to create multiple blue oceans over time, thereby continuing to deliver high growth and profits over a sustained period. The creation of blue oceans, in other words, is a product of strategy and as such is very much a product of managerial action.

The Defining Characteristics

Our research shows several common characteristics across strategic moves that create blue oceans. We found that the creators of blue oceans, in sharp contrast to companies playing by traditional rules, never use the competition as a benchmark. Instead they make it irrelevant by creating a leap in value for both buyers and the company itself. (The exhibit "Red ocean versus blue ocean strategy" compares the chief characteristics of these two strategy models.)

Perhaps the most important feature of blue ocean strategy is that it rejects the fundamental tenet of conventional strategy: that a trade-off exists between value and cost. According to this thesis, companies can either create greater value for customers at a higher cost or create reasonable value at a lower cost. In other

Red ocean versus blue ocean strategy

The imperatives for red ocean and blue ocean strategies are starkly different.

Red ocean strategy	Blue ocean strategy
Compete in existing market space.	Create uncontested market space.
Beat the competition.	Make the competition irrelevant.
Exploit existing demand.	Create and capture new demand.
Make the value/cost trade-off.	Break the value/cost trade-off.
Align the whole system of a company's activities with its strategic choice of differentiation *or* low cost.	Align the whole system of a company's activities in pursuit of differentiation *and* low cost.

words, strategy is essentially a choice between differentiation and low cost. But when it comes to creating blue oceans, the evidence shows that successful companies pursue differentiation and low cost simultaneously.

To see how this is done, let us go back to Cirque du Soleil. At the time of Cirque's debut, circuses focused on benchmarking one another and maximizing their shares of shrinking demand by tweaking traditional circus acts. This included trying to secure more and better-known clowns and lion tamers, efforts that raised circuses' cost structure without substantially altering the circus experience. The result was rising costs without rising revenues and a downward spiral in overall circus demand. Enter Cirque. Instead of following the conventional logic of outpacing the competition by offering a better solution to the given problem—creating a circus with even greater fun and thrills—it redefined the problem itself by offering people the fun and thrill of the circus *and* the intellectual sophistication and artistic richness of the theater.

In designing performances that landed both these punches, Cirque had to reevaluate the components of the traditional circus offering. What the company found was that many of the elements considered essential to the fun and thrill of the circus were unnecessary and in many cases costly. For instance, most circuses offer animal acts. These are a heavy economic burden, because circuses have to shell out not only for the animals but also for their training, medical care, housing, insurance, and transportation. Yet Cirque found that the appetite for animal shows was rapidly diminishing because of rising public concern about the treatment of circus animals and the ethics of exhibiting them.

Similarly, although traditional circuses promoted their performers as stars, Cirque realized that the public no longer thought of circus artists as stars, at least not in the movie star sense. Cirque did away with traditional three-ring shows, too. Not only did these create confusion among spectators forced to switch their attention from one ring to another, they also increased the number of performers needed, with obvious cost implications. And while aisle concession sales appeared to be a good way to generate revenue, the high prices discouraged parents from making purchases and made them feel they were being taken for a ride.

Cirque found that the lasting allure of the traditional circus came down to just three factors: the clowns, the tent, and the classic acrobatic acts. So Cirque kept the clowns, while shifting their humor away from slapstick to a more enchanting, sophisticated style. It glamorized the tent, which many circuses had abandoned in favor of rented venues. Realizing that the tent, more than anything else, captured the magic of the circus, Cirque designed this classic symbol with a glorious external finish and a high level of audience comfort. Gone were the sawdust and hard benches. Acrobats and other thrilling performers were retained, but Cirque reduced their roles and made their acts more elegant by adding artistic flair.

Even as Cirque stripped away some of the traditional circus offerings, it injected new elements drawn from the world of theater. For instance, unlike traditional circuses featuring a series of unrelated acts, each Cirque creation resembles a theater performance in that it has a theme and story line. Although the themes are intentionally vague, they bring harmony and an intellectual element to the acts. Cirque also borrows ideas from Broadway. For example, rather than putting on the traditional "once and for all" show, Cirque mounts multiple productions based on different themes and story lines. As with Broadway productions, too, each Cirque show has an original musical score, which drives the performance, lighting, and timing of the acts rather than the other way around. The productions feature abstract and spiritual dance, an idea derived from theater and ballet. By introducing these factors, Cirque has created highly sophisticated entertainments. And by staging multiple productions, Cirque gives people reason to come to the circus more often, thereby increasing revenues.

Cirque offers the best of both circus and theater. And by eliminating many of the most expensive elements of the circus, it has been able to dramatically reduce its cost structure, achieving both differentiation and low cost. (For a depiction of the economics underpinning blue ocean strategy, see the exhibit "The simultaneous pursuit of differentiation and low cost.")

By driving down costs while simultaneously driving up value for buyers, a company can achieve a leap in value for both itself and its customers. Since buyer value comes from the utility and price a company offers, and a company generates value for itself through cost structure and price, blue ocean strategy is achieved only when the whole system of a company's utility, price, and cost activities is properly aligned. It is this whole-system approach

The simultaneous pursuit of differentiation and low cost

A blue ocean is created in the region where a company's actions favorably affect both its cost structure and its value proposition to buyers. Cost savings are made from eliminating and reducing the factors an industry competes on. Buyer value is lifted by raising and creating elements the industry has never offered. Over time, costs are reduced further as scale economies kick in, due to the high sales volumes that superior value generates.

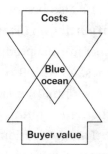

that makes the creation of blue oceans a sustainable strategy. Blue ocean strategy integrates the range of a firm's functional and operational activities.

A rejection of the trade-off between low cost and differentiation implies a fundamental change in strategic mindset—we cannot emphasize enough how fundamental a shift it is. The red ocean assumption that industry structural conditions are a given and firms are forced to compete within them is based on an intellectual worldview that academics call the *structuralist* view, or *environmental determinism*. According to this view, companies and managers are largely at the mercy of economic forces greater than themselves. Blue ocean strategies, by contrast, are based on a worldview in which market boundaries and industries can be reconstructed by the actions and beliefs of industry players. We call this the *reconstructionist* view.

The founders of Cirque du Soleil clearly did not feel constrained to act within the confines of their industry. Indeed, is Cirque really a circus with all that it has eliminated, reduced, raised, and created? Or is it theater? If it is theater, then what genre—Broadway show, opera, ballet? The magic of Cirque was created through a reconstruction of elements drawn from all of these alternatives. In the end, Cirque is none of them and a little of all of them. From within the red oceans of theater and circus, Cirque has created a blue ocean of uncontested market space that has, as yet, no name.

Barriers to Imitation

Companies that create blue oceans usually reap the benefits without credible challenges for 10 to 15 years, as was the case with Cirque du Soleil, Home Depot, Federal Express, Southwest Airlines, and CNN, to name just a few. The reason is that blue ocean strategy creates considerable economic and cognitive barriers to imitation.

For a start, adopting a blue ocean creator's business model is easier to imagine than to do. Because blue ocean creators immediately attract customers in large volumes, they are able to generate scale economies very rapidly, putting would-be imitators at an immediate and continuing cost disadvantage. The huge economies of scale in purchasing that Walmart enjoys, for example, have significantly discouraged other companies from imitating its business model. The immediate attraction of large numbers of customers can also create network externalities. The more customers eBay has online, the more attractive the auction site becomes for both sellers and buyers of wares, giving users few incentives to go elsewhere.

When imitation requires companies to make changes to their whole system of activities, organizational politics may impede a would-be competitor's ability to switch to the divergent business model of a blue ocean strategy. For instance, airlines trying to follow Southwest's example of offering the speed of air travel with the flexibility and cost of driving would have faced major revisions in routing, training, marketing, and pricing, not to mention culture. Few established airlines had the flexibility to make such extensive organizational and operating changes overnight. Imitating a whole-system approach is not an easy feat.

The cognitive barriers can be just as effective. When a company offers a leap in value, it rapidly earns brand buzz and a loyal following in the marketplace. Experience shows that even the most expensive marketing campaigns struggle to unseat a blue ocean creator. Microsoft, for example, has been trying for more than 10 years to occupy the center of the blue ocean that Intuit created with its financial software product Quicken. Despite all of its efforts and all of its investment, Microsoft has not been able to unseat Intuit as the industry leader.

In other situations, attempts to imitate a blue ocean creator conflict with the imitator's existing brand image. The Body Shop, for example, shuns top models and makes no promises of eternal youth and beauty. For the established cosmetic brands like Estée Lauder and L'Oréal, imitation was very difficult, because it would have signaled a complete invalidation of their current images, which are based on promises of eternal youth and beauty.

A Consistent Pattern

While our conceptual articulation of the pattern may be new, blue ocean strategy has always existed, whether or not companies have been conscious of the fact. Just consider the striking parallels between the Cirque du Soleil theater-circus experience and Ford's creation of the Model T.

At the end of the 19th century, the automobile industry was small and unattractive. More than 500 automakers in America competed in turning out handmade luxury cars that cost around $1,500 and were enormously *un*popular with all but the very rich. Anticar activists tore up roads, ringed parked cars with barbed wire, and organized boycotts of car-driving businessmen and politicians. Woodrow Wilson caught the spirit of the times when he said in 1906 that "nothing has spread socialistic feeling more than the automobile." He called it "a picture of the arrogance of wealth."

Instead of trying to beat the competition and steal a share of existing demand from other automakers, Ford reconstructed the industry boundaries of cars and horse-drawn carriages to create a blue ocean. At the time, horse-drawn carriages were the primary means of local transportation across America. The carriage had two distinct advantages over cars. Horses could easily negotiate the bumps and mud that stymied cars—especially in rain and snow—on the nation's ubiquitous dirt roads. And horses and carriages were much easier to maintain than the luxurious autos of the time, which frequently broke down, requiring expert repairmen who were expensive and in short supply. It was Henry Ford's understanding of these advantages that showed him how he could break away from the competition and unlock enormous untapped demand.

Ford called the Model T the car "for the great multitude, constructed of the best materials." Like Cirque, the Ford Motor Company made the competition irrelevant. Instead of creating fashionable, customized cars for weekends in the countryside, a luxury few could justify, Ford built a car that, like the horse-drawn carriage, was for everyday use. The Model T came in just one color, black, and there were few optional extras. It was reliable and durable, designed to travel effortlessly over dirt roads in rain, snow, or sunshine. It was easy to use and fix. People could learn to drive it in a day. And like Cirque, Ford went outside the industry for a price point, looking at horse-drawn carriages ($400), not other autos. In 1908, the first Model T cost $850; in 1909, the price dropped to $609, and by 1924 it was down to $290. In this way, Ford converted buyers of horse-drawn carriages into car buyers—just as Cirque turned theatergoers into circusgoers. Sales of the Model T boomed. Ford's market share surged from 9% in 1908 to 61% in 1921, and by 1923, a majority of American households had a car.

Even as Ford offered the mass of buyers a leap in value, the company also achieved the lowest cost structure in the industry, much as Cirque did later. By keeping the cars highly standardized with limited options and interchangeable parts, Ford was able to scrap the prevailing manufacturing system in which cars were constructed by skilled craftsmen who swarmed around one workstation and built a car piece by piece from start to finish. Ford's revolutionary assembly line replaced craftsmen with unskilled laborers, each of whom worked quickly and efficiently on one small task. This allowed Ford to make a car in just four days—21 days was the industry norm—creating huge cost savings.

. . .

Blue and red oceans have always coexisted and always will. Practical reality, therefore, demands that companies understand the strategic logic of both types of oceans. At present, competing in red oceans dominates the field of strategy in theory and in practice, even as businesses' need to create blue oceans intensifies. It is time to even the scales in the field of strategy with a better balance of efforts across both oceans. For although blue ocean strategists have always existed, for the most part their strategies have been largely unconscious. But once corporations realize that the strategies for creating and capturing blue oceans have a different underlying logic from red ocean strategies, they will be able to create many more blue oceans in the future.

Originally published in October 2004 2011. Reprint R0410D

Strategic Choices Need to Be Made Simultaneously, Not Sequentially

by Roger L. Martin

T he CEO of a large Australian company called me to relay a particular strategy-development problem his firm was facing and ask for my advice. The company was an eager user of my "cascading choices" framework for strategy, which I have used for decades and written about extensively, most prominently in *Playing to Win*, the 2013 book I wrote with friend and colleague A.G. Lafley.

My Australian friend explained that each of his five business-unit presidents was using the Strategy Choice Cascade and that all of them had gotten stuck in the same place. They had chosen a Winning Aspiration and had settled on a Where to Play choice. But all of them were stuck at the How to Win box.

"It's no surprise," I told my friend, "that they have gotten stuck. It's because they considered Where to Play without reference to How to Win."

The strategy choice cascade

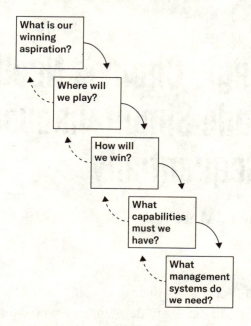

Source: *Playing to Win: How Strategy Really Works*, by A.G. Lafley and Roger L. Martin (Boston: Harvard Business Review Press, 2013).

I've heard variants of this over and over. Although I have always emphasized that these five choices have to link together and reinforce one another (hence the arrows flowing back and forth between the boxes), it has become clear to me that I haven't done a good enough job of making this point, especially as it relates to the choices of Where to Play and How to Win.

The challenge here is that they are linked, and *together* they are the heart of strategy; without a great Where to Play and How to Win combination, you can't possibly have a worthwhile strategy. Of course, Where to Play and How to Win have to link with and reinforce an inspiring Winning Aspiration. And Capabilities

Idea in Brief

The Challenge

Many organizations struggle with strategic planning because they make key decisions in isolation. This approach often leads to misaligned strategies that fail to deliver optimal results.

The Solution

Executives must make choices about Where to Play and How to Win simultaneously, since their strategic elements need to reinforce one another to create a cohesive and powerful approach. By doing so, leaders can develop matched sets of decisions that align with the organization's overall goals and competitive context.

The Payoff

Organizations that implement this integrated strategy-making process are better positioned to navigate complex environments, respond to market changes, and execute their strategies with greater precision and impact.

and Management Systems act as reality checks on the Where to Play and How to Win choices. If you can't identify sets of Capabilities and Management Systems that you currently have, or can reasonably build, to make the Where to Play and How to Win choices come to fruition, then what you have is a fantasy, not a strategy.

Many people ask me why Capabilities and Management Systems are part of strategy when they are really elements of execution. That is yet another manifestation of the widespread, artificial, and unhelpful attempt to distinguish between choices that are "strategic" and ones that are "executional" or "tactical." Remember that, regardless of the name you give them, these choices are critical parts of the integrated set of five choices necessary to successfully guide the actions of an organization.

I had to tell my Australian friend that locking and loading on Where to Play choices, rather than setting the table for a great discussion of How to Win, actually makes it virtually impossible to have a productive consideration of How to Win. That is because no meaningful Where to Play choice exists outside the context of a particular How to Win plan. An infinite number of Where to Play choices are possible and equally meritorious—before considering each one's How to Win. In other words, there aren't inherently strong and weak Where to Play choices. They are only strong or weak in the context of a particular How to Win choice. Therefore, making lists of Where to Play options before considering How to Win options has zero value in strategy.

For example, Uber made a Where to Play choice that included China because it's a huge and important market. But being huge and important didn't make that choice inherently meritorious. It would have been worthy only if there had been a clear How to Win as well—which it appears there never was. Microsoft made a Where to Play choice to get into smartphone hardware (with its acquisition of Nokia's handset business) because it was a huge and growing market, seemingly adjacent to Microsoft's own. But it had no useful conception of how that would be twinned with a How to Win choice—and it lost spectacularly. Procter & Gamble made a Where to Play choice to get into the huge, profitable, and growing pharmaceutical business with the acquisition of Norwich Eaton, in 1982. While it performed decently, P&G divested the business in 2009 because, in those nearly two decades, it came to realize that it could play but never win in that still-exciting Where to Play.

Moreover, no meaningful How to Win plan exists outside the context of a particular Where to Play choice. Despite what many think, there are not generically great ways to win—for example, being a first mover or a fast follower or a branded player or a cost leader. All How to Win options are useful, or not, depending on the Where to Play with which they are paired. A How to Win choice based on superior scale is not going to be useful if the Where to Play choice is to concentrate on a narrow niche—because that would undermine an attempted scale advantage.

Undoubtedly, Uber thought its How to Win plan—having an easy-to-use ride-hailing app for users twinned with a vehicle for making extra money for drivers—would work well in any Where to Play. But it didn't work in the Where to Play of China. It turned out that Uber's How to Win had a lot to do with building a first-mover advantage in markets like the United States; when Uber was a late entrant, the Where to Play wasn't a simple extension, and it exited after losing convincingly to first mover DiDi. Perhaps Microsoft felt that its How to Win of having strong corporate relationships and a huge installed base of software users would extend nicely into smartphones, but it most assuredly didn't. As a Canadian, I can't help but recall the many Canadian retailers with powerful How to Wins here (Tim Hortons, Canadian Tire, Jean Coutu) that simply didn't translate to a Where to Play in the United States. Perhaps there is some solace, however, in retailer Target's disastrous attempt to extend its U.S. How to Win into the Canadian Where to Play—turnabout is, I guess, fair play.

The only productive, intelligent way to generate possibilities for strategy is to consider *matched pairs* of Where to Play and How to Win options. Generate a variety of pairs and then ask about each set:

- Can it be linked to an inspiring, attractive Winning Aspiration?

- Do we currently have, or can we reasonably build, the Capabilities that would be necessary to win where we would play?

- Can we create the Management Systems that would need to be in place to support the building and maintenance of the necessary Capabilities?

Those Where to Play and How to Win possibilities for which these questions can plausibly be answered in the affirmative should be taken forward for more consideration and exploration. For the great success stories of our time, the tight match of Where to Play and How to Win is immediately obvious. USAA sells insurance only to military personnel, veterans, and their families and tailors its offerings brilliantly and tightly to the needs of those in that sphere—so much so that its customer satisfaction scores are off the charts. Vanguard sells index mutual funds/exchange-traded funds to customers who don't believe that active management is helpful to the performance of their investments. With that tight Where to Play, it can win by working to achieve the lowest cost position in the business. Google wins by organizing the world's information, but to do that it has to play across the broadest swath of search.

It doesn't matter whether the strategic question is to aim broadly or narrowly, or to pursue low costs or differentiation. What does matter is that the answers are a perfectly matched pair.

Adapted from hbr.org, April 3, 2017. Reprint H03K4Y

Put Purpose at the Core of Your Strategy

**by Thomas W. Malnight,
Ivy Buche, and Charles Dhanaraj**

ight years ago we launched a global study of high growth in companies, investigating the importance of three strategies known to drive it: creating new markets, serving broader stakeholder needs, and changing the rules of the game. What we found surprised us. Although each of those approaches did boost growth at the organizations we studied, there was a fourth driver we hadn't considered at all: purpose.

Companies have long been encouraged to build purpose into what they do. But usually it's talked about as an add-on—a way to create shared value, improve employee morale and commitment, give back to the community, and help the environment. But as we worked with the high-growth companies in our study and beyond, we began to recognize that many of them had moved purpose from the periphery of their strategy to its core—where, with committed leadership and financial investment, they had used it to generate sustained profitable growth, stay relevant in a rapidly changing world, and deepen ties with their stakeholders.

Two Critical Roles

In the course of our research, we talked to scores of C-level executives. They worked at 28 companies—in the United States, Europe, and India—that had had an average compound annual growth rate of 30% or more in the previous five years. What we learned from those conversations was that purpose played two important strategic roles: It helped companies *redefine the playing field*, and it allowed them to *reshape the value proposition*. And that, in turn, enabled them to overcome the challenges of slowing growth and declining profitability.

Role 1: Redefining the playing field

What's a key difference between low-growth and high-growth companies? The former spend most of their time fighting for market share on one playing field, which naturally restricts their growth potential. And because most aggressive battles take place in industries that are slowing down, gains in market share come at a high cost, often eroding profits and competitive advantage as offerings become commoditized.

High-growth companies, by contrast, don't feel limited to their current playing field. Instead, they think about whole ecosystems, where connected interests and relationships among multiple stakeholders create more opportunities. But these firms don't approach ecosystems haphazardly. They let purpose be their guide.

Consider the different strategies adopted by the two leading companies in the pet-food industry: Nestlé Purina PetCare, the

Idea in Brief

The Challenge

Companies pursuing high growth tend to follow three well-known strategies: creating new markets, serving broader stakeholder needs, and changing the rules of the game. But there's another critical growth driver: purpose.

The Insight

Many companies consider purpose merely an add-on to their strategy, but the most successful companies put it at the core, using it to redefine the playing field and reshape their value propositions.

The Benefits

A purpose-driven strategy helps companies overcome the challenges of slowing growth and declining profits. It also helps with the soft side of management: the people-related aspects of running a business, which so often prove to be the undoing of leaders.

largest player in North America; and Mars Petcare, the global leader. The companies have defined very similar purposes for themselves—"Better with pets" (Purina) and "A better world for pets" (Mars Petcare)—and both want to develop new products that will help customers improve their pets' health. But Purina has continued to focus on the pet-food playing field and is applying purpose in some inspiring social initiatives, whereas Mars Petcare is using purpose to propel its expansion in the broader field of pet health.

Mars Petcare, which had established a foothold in pet health with the acquisition of Banfield Pet Hospital in 2007, decided to build its presence in that arena by buying two other veterinary services: BluePearl in 2015 and VCA in 2017. Then in 2018 Mars Petcare entered the European veterinary market, buying the Swedish company AniCura, which has operations in seven

European countries, and the British company Linnaeus. Those acquisitions helped Mars Petcare become Mars Inc.'s largest and fastest-growing business division.

In moving deeper into this larger ecosystem, Mars Petcare did more than just capitalize on a burgeoning industry. It also shifted its orientation beyond products to services, a radical change for an asset-heavy company that for 75 years had relied on the production and sale of goods. To succeed, the company had to build completely different core competencies and devise a new organizational structure. Many companies in this dangerously open-ended situation might have flailed, but Mars Petcare did not. It was able to pull off a transformation because it ensured that every move it made was aligned with the same core purpose. And it's not done yet: The company is now bringing that sense of purpose to efforts to expand into pet-activity monitoring with "smart" collars.

Another company that has used purpose to redefine the playing field, this time in the industrial sector, is the Finnish oil-refining firm Neste. For more than six decades Neste, founded in 1948, operated a business focused almost entirely on crude oil, but by 2009 it was struggling. The market was glutted, oil prices had dropped sharply, margins were falling, and the EU had passed new carbon-emissions legislation. During the previous two years, the company's market value had shrunk by 50%.

Fighting those headwinds, the executive team, led by Neste's new CEO, Matti Lievonen, realized that the company could no longer survive on its traditional playing field. It would have to look for new opportunities in the larger ecosystem. Renewable energy could be a key driver of growth, they realized. Their purpose, they decided, should be to develop sustainable sources of energy that would help reduce emissions, and everything they did would be guided by a simple idea: "Creating responsible choices every day."

It's common for major oil companies to nod to sustainability in some way, but Lievonen quickly proved that Neste meant business, launching a bold transformation that would become a seven-year journey. Employees, customers, and investors all initially resisted the change, but Lievonen and his team were undaunted. They made major investments in infrastructure, innovated renewable technologies, focused on converting customers to green energy solutions, and, most important, engineered a fundamental change in the company's culture.

The process wasn't easy. When Lievonen was just three months into his tenure, a leading economic magazine in Finland published an article saying that he should be fired. He soldiered on, however, and by 2015 Neste had established itself as the world's largest producer of renewable fuels derived from waste and residues. A year later its comparable operating profits from renewables would surpass those of its oil-products business. In 2017 the company took yet another step by actively researching and promoting the use of waste feedstock from new sources such as algae oil, microbial oil, and tall oil pitch.

Role 2: Reshaping the value proposition

When confronted with eroding margins in a rapidly commodifying world, companies often enhance their value propositions by innovating products, services, or business models. That can bring some quick wins, but it's a transactional approach geared toward prevailing in the current arena. Because a purpose-driven approach facilitates growth in new ecosystems, it allows companies to broaden their mission, create a holistic value proposition, and deliver lifetime benefits to customers.

Companies can make this shift in three main ways: by responding to trends, building on trust, and focusing on pain points.

Responding to trends. In line with its purpose of "contributing to a safer society," Sweden's Securitas AB, a security company with 370,000 employees, has traditionally offered physical guarding services. But in the early 2010s its CEO at the time, Alf Göransson, saw that globalization, urbanization, and the increasingly networked business landscape were all changing the nature of risk—for people, operations, and business continuity. At the same time, labor was becoming more expensive, and new technologies were becoming cheaper. Given those developments, Göransson decided that Securitas could no longer "simply sell man-hours." Instead, the company had to explore new ways of using electronics to provide security. This shift, Göransson understood, was not a threat to the existing business but an opportunity to grow—as indeed it has proved to be.

In 2018 the company decided to go a step further and reshape its value proposition from reactive to predictive security, a plan that once again built on the company's core purpose. Under the leadership of Göransson's successor, Magnus Ahlqvist, the firm strengthened its electronic security business by acquiring a number of companies, investing heavily in modernizing and integrating back-office systems, and training its guards in remote surveillance, digital reporting, and efficient response. That allowed Securitas to offer bundled, customized security solutions—encompassing physical guarding, electronic security, and risk management—that provided a much-enhanced level of protection at an optimized cost. By expanding its value proposition in this way, Securitas has been able to strengthen client relationships and significantly increase its margins for the solutions business. From 2012 to 2018 the company's sales of security solutions and electronic security also increased, from 6% of total revenue to 20%.

Building on trust. When Mahindra Finance, the financial services arm of the Mahindra Group, a $20 billion Indian conglomerate, wanted to define its value proposition, it looked to its parent company's longtime purpose-driven strategy of improving customers' lives—encapsulated in 2010 by the simple motto "Rise." It's a word that the company's third-generation leader, Anand Mahindra, expects will inspire employees to accept no limits, think alternatively, and drive positive change.

In keeping with that strategy, Mahindra Finance decided to target its core offering, vehicle financing, to rural areas, where it could—as Rajeev Dubey, the group head of HR, put it to us—"address the unmet needs of underserved customers in an underpenetrated market."

That meant that the company had to figure out how to determine the creditworthiness of customers who were mostly poor, illiterate, and unbanked, with no identity documents, no collateral, and cash flows that were often impacted by monsoons. To do that, the company had to develop completely new ways to handle loan design, repayment terms, customer approval, branch locations, and disbursement and collection in cash. Not only that, but it had to figure out how to recruit workers who could speak local dialects, assess local situations, and operate under a decentralized model of decision-making.

Remarkably, the company managed to do all those things and established a preliminary level of trust with its customers. It then stretched its value proposition to help farmers and other customers obtain insurance for their tractors, lives, and health. In a country where insurance penetration is abysmally low (about 3.5%), this was no small feat, especially since rural residents didn't easily part with any minuscule monthly surplus they had, even if it was to secure their livelihood.

Then Mahindra Finance extended its purpose-driven efforts to housing finance, another arena in which it recognized that it could help its rural customers rise above their circumstances. For most of those people, securing loans for housing was difficult in the extreme. Banks offered loans at an interest rate of about 10% but demanded documentation most rural residents couldn't provide. Moneylenders offered instant financing but charged interest rates of about 40%. Recognizing an opportunity, Mahindra Finance decided to play at the intermediate level, offering customized home loans at rates of about 14%, an option that appealed to its growing base of customers. And when some of those customers developed successful small agribusinesses, they began looking for working-capital loans, equipment loans, project finance, and so on—more unmet needs that Mahindra Finance could address. So it extended its value proposition again, into the small-to-medium-enterprise arena, offering finance and asset-management services.

Throughout its expansion, Mahindra Finance was guided by its goal of helping rural citizens improve their lives. The company identified and committed itself to value propositions that allowed it to deepen its relationship with its customers, which in turn created additional streams of revenue and profits. Today Mahindra Finance is India's largest rural nonbanking financial company, serving 50% of villages and 6 million customers.

Focusing on pain points. We've already seen how Mars Petcare's health care value proposition led to direct connections with pet owners at multiple touchpoints. Having established them, the company looked for other ways to create "a better world for pets." How could it come up with a value proposition that would make pet ownership a seamless, convenient, and attractive experience?

The answer was by investing in technology to help address one of the biggest concerns of pet owners: *preventing* health problems. In 2016 the company acquired Whistle, the San Francisco–based maker of a connected collar for activity monitoring and location tracking—a kind of Fitbit for dogs. Teaming the device up with its Banfield Pet Hospital unit, the company launched the Pet Insight Project, a three-year longitudinal study that aims to enroll 200,000 dogs in the United States. By combining machine learning, data science, and deep veterinary expertise, the project seeks to understand when behavior may signal a change in a pet's health and how owners can partner with their veterinarians on individualized diagnostics and treatments for their pets.

Developing a Purpose

Leaders and companies that have effectively defined corporate purpose typically have done so with one of two approaches: *retrospective* or *prospective*.

The retrospective approach builds on a firm's existing reason for being. It requires that you look back, codify organizational and cultural DNA, and make sense of the firm's past. The focus of the discovery process is internal. Where have we come from? How did we get here? What makes us unique to all stakeholders? Where does our DNA open up future opportunities we believe in? These are the kinds of questions leaders have to ask.

Anand Mahindra very successfully employed this tactic at the Mahindra Group. First he looked back at his 30 years at the

Is Purpose at the Core of Your Strategy?

Not unless you answer yes to all five questions below.

	Yes	No
1. Does purpose contribute to increasing your company's growth and profitability today?	❑	❑
2. Does purpose significantly influence your strategic decisions and investment choices?	❑	❑
3. Does purpose shape your core value proposition?	❑	❑
4. Does purpose affect how you build and manage your organizational capabilities?	❑	❑
5. Is purpose on the agenda of your leadership team every time you meet?	❑	❑

company and at the values that had guided him as its leader. Then he delved into the psyche of the organization by conducting internal surveys of managers at all levels. He also did ethnographic research in seven countries to identify themes that resonated with his company's multinational, cross-cultural employee base. The process took three years, but ultimately Mahindra arrived at "Rise," which, he realized, had been fundamental to the company from its inception. "'Rise' is not a clever tagline," he has said. "We were already living and operating this way."

The prospective approach, on the other hand, reshapes your reason for being. It requires you to look forward, take stock of the broader ecosystem in which you want to work, and assess your potential for impact in it. The idea is to make sense of the future and then start gearing your organization for it. The focus is external, and leaders have to ask a different set of questions: Where can we go? Which trends affect our business? What new needs, opportunities, and challenges lie ahead? What role can we play that will open up future opportunities for ourselves that we believe in?

The prospective approach can be particularly useful for new CEOs. In 2018, when Magnus Ahlqvist took charge at Securitas, he spearheaded a "purpose workstream" to capture aspirations for the company from the ground up. He asked all his business-unit leaders to run "listening workshops" (with groups of employees from diverse functions, levels, age groups, genders, and backgrounds), which were held over six months. At the end of that period, the findings were collated and analyzed. Among the discoveries: Employees had a vision of transforming the company from a *service provider* to a *trusted adviser*. That shift would require anticipating and responding to security issues instead of relying on the legacy methods of observing and reporting. So employee input helped executives refine the firm's predictive-security strategy.

Implementing a Purpose-Driven Strategy

Our research shows that a compelling purpose clarifies what a company stands for, provides an impetus for action, and is aspirational. But some purpose statements are so generic that they could apply to any company (like Nissan's "Enriching people's lives"), while others provide only a narrow description of the company's existing businesses (like Wells Fargo's "We want to satisfy our customers' financial needs and help them succeed financially"). Even if organizations do manage to define their purpose well, they often don't properly translate it into action—or do anything at all to fulfill it. In those cases, the purpose becomes nothing more than nice-sounding words on a wall.

Leaders need to think hard about how to make purpose central to their strategy. The two best tactics for doing that are to *transform the leadership agenda* and to *disseminate purpose throughout the organization.*

Consider Mars Petcare again. In 2015 its president, Poul Weihrauch, significantly altered the composition and focus of the leadership team. Its new collective agenda, he declared, would go beyond the performance of individual businesses; it would include generating "multiplier effects" among the businesses (such as between pet food and pet health) and increasing their contributions to creating a better world for pets.

In keeping with that principle, Weihrauch had the company adopt an "outside-in" approach to meeting stakeholder needs. As part of this effort, in 2018 Mars Petcare launched two new programs to support startups innovating in pet care: Leap Venture Studio, a business accelerator formed in partnership with Michelson Found Animals and R/GA; and Companion Fund, a $100 million venture-capital fund in partnership with Digitalis Ventures. In announcing these initiatives, the company declared that its ambition was "to become a partner of choice for everyone willing to change the rules of the game in pet care."

Revising a leadership agenda and restructuring an organization are arguably easier at a privately held company like Mars Petcare than at a publicly held one. But Finland's Neste is public, with a major stake held by the government, and it has managed to do both things very effectively.

Neste faced an uphill battle when it decided to move into renewables. The company had to build new capabilities while confronting strong opposition from many employees who didn't buy into the change in direction. About 10% of them left during the first year of the strategy's implementation. Painful as it was, it proved to be a positive development, since the company could not have forged ahead with people who didn't believe in its new purpose.

And forge ahead it did. Neste put in place a new top management team, mobilized its 1,500 R&D engineers, innovated patented renewable technology, and invested €2 billion in building new refineries.

The shift also raised a big question for Neste. How could it change its organizational mindset from *volume* to *value* selling—which entailed convincing customers that its clean fuels would be better for them in the long run? That shift meant going beyond wholesalers to work directly with the distributors and even the distributors' customers. The new leadership team realized that a much higher level of collaboration among business segments and functions was imperative. Winning deals was no longer the sole responsibility of the sales department. The expertise of the whole organization—product knowledge, marketing, finance, taxation—would be required to understand the specific needs of customers like airlines and bus fleets. So Neste engineered a major reorganization and created a matrix structure, in the process rotating about 25% of senior managers and about 50% of upper professionals into new positions. Targets and incentive plans became cross-functional, designed to build capabilities both within and across businesses. And at every step, purpose helped everybody in the company understand the "why" (the business environment's increasing emphasis on sustainability), the "what" (value-creation programs offering renewable solutions to customers, which in turn generated higher margins for

Neste), and the "how" (changing from a sales organization to a key-account management model with dedicated people responsible for strategic customers).

The process worked. Neste is now a leader in the renewables industry, and the world is starting to pay attention. In 2015, for example, Google and UPS began partnering with the company to reduce their carbon emissions, as did several cities in California, among them San Francisco and Oakland. In 2018, *Forbes* ranked Neste second on its Global 100 list of the world's most-sustainable companies.

Benefits on the Soft Side

Purpose can also help with the soft side of management—the people-related aspects of running a business, which so often prove to be the undoing of leaders. By putting purpose at the core of strategy, firms can realize three specific benefits: more-unified organizations, more-motivated stakeholders, and a broader positive impact on society.

Unifying the organization. When companies pursue dramatic change and move into larger ecosystems, as both Mars Petcare and Securitas have done, it's unsettling for employees. Why does a pet-food company need to develop a platform to support technology startups? Why does an on-site guarding company want to provide electronic security services that could, over time, make the physical presence of guards redundant? Purpose helps employees understand the whys and get on board with the new direction.

Motivating stakeholders. According to the Edelman trust barometer, distrust of government, businesses, the media, and NGOs is now pervasive. At the same time, more than ever, employees, especially millennials, want to work for organizations that can be trusted to contribute to a higher cause. And when customers, suppliers, and other stakeholders see that a company has a strong higher purpose, they are more likely to trust it and be more motivated to interact with it.

Broadening impact. Strategy involves exploring some fundamental questions. Why are we in this business? What value can we bring? What role does my unit play within the bigger portfolio? Purpose creates a basis for answering those questions and defining how each unit will contribute to the organization and to society as a whole. This focus on collective objectives, in turn, opens up many more opportunities to improve growth and profitability today and in the future.

· · ·

The approach to purpose that we're recommending cannot be a one-off effort. Leaders need to constantly assess how purpose can guide strategy, and they need to be willing to adjust or redefine this relationship as conditions change. That demands a new kind of sustained focus, but the advantages it can confer are legion.

Originally published in September–October 2019. Reprint R1905D

Take the Bias Out of Strategy Decisions

by Freek Vermeulen

Some time ago, a London friend of mine was diagnosed with a severe medical condition that required urgent yet complex surgery. The condition is rare, but fortunately there were several specialists in both Germany and France who had each treated hundreds of cases during their careers. When it comes to specialist operations, experience is key, so my friend planned to visit each of them and then make a decision.

However, when I spoke to him again, he had decided where he was going to have the operation: in the hospital in his hometown in Spain. I was surprised; there was no specialist in that hospital. But he explained that he had flown to his home country for another opinion and that the local surgeon had made a good impression and was very pleasant. Moreover, my friend added, after the surgery he would have to stay in the hospital for two weeks—and it would be nice to do that near his family.

I was stunned. My friend is a rational guy, in charge of a large company. I have no doubt that, if he had been helping me make this decision, he would have immediately recommended that I go to a real specialist, wherever they were in the world. He would have told me that wherever I spent the two weeks in a hospital bed and whether the surgeon was a good conversationalist were both immaterial factors. But when making this important decision for himself, emotional considerations took over. And unfortunately, the initial operation was unsuccessful, and my friend had to travel abroad to see a specialist anyway.

Many of us would make the same irrational decision, with the same troubling consequences. Whether for a personal choice or a strategic business decision, emotions often overrule objectivity. After all, executives are only human too. It is precisely because strategic choices are such important ones, loaded with anxiety and uncertainty, that when faced with a major decision people start to follow their heart, rely on intuition and gut feeling, overestimate their chances of success, and let their commitment escalate.

Good leaders don't allow their emotional bonds to cloud their judgment. Sound strategy requires objectivity. What can executives do to remain objective when it comes to strategic choices such as which businesses to enter, what to focus on and invest in, or when to pull the plug and abandon a course of action?

Make decision rules beforehand

One way to remain objective is to develop and set a clear decision rule in advance, when there is nothing concrete to decide yet. When Intel was still focused on producing memory chips, Stanford professor Robert Burgelman documented that CEO Gordon Moore had emotional trouble abandoning that product in favor of the much more profitable microprocessors—even though the chips were costing the company money—because memory chips had "made the company." (Moore famously declared, "But that would be like Ford getting out of cars!")[1] Yet the change

Idea in Brief

The Challenge
Strategic decisions are often influenced by cognitive biases, leading to suboptimal outcomes. These biases can cloud judgment, distort perceptions, and result in decisions that do not align with the organization's best interests.

The Solution
By understanding how overconfidence, anchoring, and other biases affect decision-making, and implementing structured decision-making processes to reduce their influence, leaders can take steps to minimize the impact of bias. Techniques such as premortem analysis and scenario planning can help encourage objective evaluation and critical thinking.

The Payoff
Organizations that effectively address cognitive biases in their strategic decision-making processes are more likely to see improved strategic alignment, enhanced organizational performance, and a stronger competitive position.

ultimately happened because Intel relied on its so-called production capacity allocation rule.

Gordon Moore and Andy Grove, well before this actual dilemma became relevant, had put together a formula—the production capacity allocation rule—to decide how to prioritize products in their manufacturing plant. When top management had emotional difficulty deciding to abandon memory chips, microprocessors were automatically receiving more production capacity anyway, because middle managers sturdily followed the rule that they had been given before. Because top management had made the decision of what sort of product should receive production priority well before it became a concrete issue, the strategic choice became detached from their emotion of the moment.

Tap into the wisdom of your crowd

A second method to depersonalize difficult decisions is to avoid leaving pivotal choices in the hands of just one or a few individuals—usually top managers—but instead to tap into the wisdom of the company's internal crowd. When I asked Tony Cohen (the former CEO of FremantleMedia, producer of television programs such as *The X Factor, American Idol, Family Feud,* and *The Price Is Right*) how he decided what new programs to invest in, he replied, "I don't make that decision." He resisted making such crucial investment decisions himself; instead he designed an internal system that identified the most promising ideas by tapping into the collective opinion of his television executives across the world.

For example, every year he organized the Fremantle Market, an internal meeting in London where Fremantle executives from all over the world presented their new ideas (usually in the form of a trial episode). Subsequently, an internal licensing system ensured that prototype programs that many of the executives liked automatically got funded. If an idea did not receive much support, it would not receive any investment—even if Cohen himself happened to like it. That way, the decision did not rest in the hands of any individual, no matter how senior.

The revolving-door approach

Finally, a valuable technique is to explicitly adopt an outside perspective. Regarding his debates with Moore about whether to abandon dynamic random-access memory (DRAM), Grove said, "I recall going to see Gordon and asking him what a new management would do if we were replaced. The answer was clear: Get out of DRAMs. So I suggested to Gordon that we go through the revolving door, come back in, and just do it ourselves." Taking the perspective of an outsider—a new CEO, private equity firm, or turnaround manager—can help you see things more clearly. Research shows, for example, that people are very bad at estimating the time it will take them to complete a project (such as writing an assignment or refurbishing a house), but they are good at estimating it for someone else.[2] Asking someone to take a third-person perspective has been shown to help objectivize a process, making their judgment more accurate and realistic.

When making important strategic decisions that are going to decide our fates and those of our organizations, it is important to avoid letting emotions and personal preferences cloud our judgment. Emotional commitment can be good, but not if it gets in the way of sound decision-making. Depersonalizing decision-making may sound cold or aloof, but it's the best way to ensure a better outcome—for ourselves and our companies.

Adapted from hbr.org, January 15, 2014. Reprint H00MP3

Transient Advantage

by Rita McGrath

S trategy is stuck. For too long the business world has been obsessed with the notion of building a sustainable competitive advantage. That idea is at the core of most strategy textbooks; it forms the basis of Warren Buffett's investment strategy; it's central to the success of companies on the "most admired" lists. I'm not arguing that it's a bad idea—obviously, it's marvelous to compete in a way that others can't imitate. And even today there are companies that create a strong position and defend it for extended periods of time—firms such as GE, IKEA, Unilever, Tsingtao Brewery, and Swiss Re. But it's now rare for a company to maintain a truly lasting advantage. Competitors and customers have become too unpredictable, and industries too amorphous. The forces at work here are familiar: the digital revolution, a "flat" world, fewer barriers to entry, globalization.

Strategy *is* still useful in turbulent industries like consumer electronics, fast-moving consumer goods, television, publishing, photography, and ... well, you get the idea. Leaders in these businesses can compete effectively—but not by sticking to the same old playbook. In a world where a competitive advantage often evaporates in less than a year, companies can't afford to spend months at a time crafting a single long-term strategy. To stay ahead, they need to constantly start new strategic initiatives, building and exploiting many *transient competitive advantages* at once. Though individually temporary, these advantages, as a portfolio, can keep companies in the lead over the long run. Firms that have figured this out—such as Milliken & Company, a U.S.-based textiles and chemicals company; Cognizant, a global IT services company; and Brambles, a logistics company based in Australia—have abandoned the assumption that stability in business is the norm. They don't even think it should be a goal. Instead, they work to spark continuous change, avoiding dangerous rigidity. They view strategy differently—as more fluid, more customer-centric, less industry-bound. And the ways they formulate it—the lens they use to define the competitive playing field, their methods for evaluating new business opportunities, their approach to innovation—are different as well.

I'm hardly the first person to write about how fast-moving competition changes strategy; indeed, I'm building on the work of Ian MacMillan (a longtime coauthor), Kathleen Eisenhardt, Yves Doz, George Stalk, Mikko Kosonen, Richard D'Aveni, Paul Nunes, and others. However, the thinking in this area—and the reality on the ground—has reached an inflection point. The field of strategy needs to acknowledge what a multitude of practitioners already know: Sustainable competitive advantage is now the exception, not the rule. Transient advantage is the new normal.

Idea in Brief

The dominant idea in the field of strategy—that success consists of establishing a unique competitive position, sustained for long periods of time—is no longer relevant for most businesses. They need to embrace the notion of transient advantage instead, learning to launch new strategic initiatives again and again, and creating a portfolio of advantages that can be built quickly and abandoned just as rapidly. Success will require a new set of operational capabilities.

The Anatomy of a Transient Advantage

Any competitive advantage—whether it lasts two seasons or two decades—goes through the same life cycle. (See "The wave of transient advantage.") But when advantages are fleeting, firms must rotate through the cycle much more quickly and more often, so they need a deeper understanding of the early and late stages than they would if they were able to maintain one strong position for many years.

The wave of transient advantage

Companies in high-velocity industries must learn to cycle rapidly through the stages of competitive advantage. They also need the capacity to develop and manage a pipeline of initiatives, since many will be short-lived.

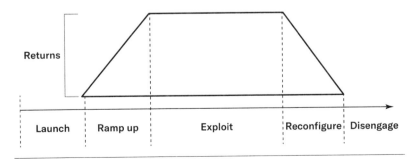

A competitive advantage begins with a *launch* process, in which the organization identifies an opportunity and mobilizes resources to capitalize on it. In this phase a company needs people who are capable of filling in blank sheets of paper with ideas, who are comfortable with experimentation and iteration, and who probably get bored with the kind of structure required to manage a large, complex organization.

In the next phase, *ramp up*, the business idea is brought to scale. This period calls for people who can assemble the right resources at the right time with the right quality and deliver on the promise of the idea.

Then, if a firm is fortunate, it begins a period of *exploitation*, in which it captures profits and share, and forces competitors to react. At this point a company needs people who are good at M&A, analytical decision-making, and efficiency. Traditional established companies have plenty of talent with this skill set.

Often, the very success of the initiative spawns competition, weakening the advantage. So the firm has to *reconfigure* what it's doing to keep the advantage fresh. For reconfigurations, a firm needs people who aren't afraid to radically rethink business models or resources.

In some cases the advantage is completely eroded, compelling the company to begin a *disengagement* process in which resources are extracted and reallocated to the next-generation advantage. To manage this process, you need people who can be candid and tough-minded and can make emotionally difficult decisions.

For sensible reasons, companies with any degree of maturity tend to be oriented toward the exploitation phase of the life cycle. But as I've suggested, they need different skills, metrics, and people to manage the tasks inherent in each stage of an advantage's development. And if they're creating a pipeline of competitive advantages, the challenge is even more complex, because they'll need to orchestrate many activities that are inconsistent with one another.

Milliken & Company is a fascinating example of an organization that managed to overcome the competitive forces that annihilated its industry (albeit over a longer time period than some companies today will be granted). By 1991 virtually all of Milliken's traditional competitors had vanished, victims of a surge in global competition that moved the entire business of textile manufacturing to Asia. In Milliken, ones sees very clearly the pattern of entering new, more promising arenas while disengaging from older, exhausted ones. Ultimately, the company exited most of its textile lines, but it did not do so suddenly. It gradually shut down American plants, starting in the 1980s and continuing through 2009. (Every effort was made, as best I can tell, to reallocate workers who might have suffered as a result.) At the same time the company was investing in international expansion, new technologies, and new markets, including forays into new arenas to which its capabilities provided access. As a result, a company that had been largely focused on textiles and chemicals through the 1960s, and advanced materials and flameproof products through the 1990s, had become a leader in specialty materials and high-IP specialty chemicals by the 2000s.

Facing the Brutal Truth

In a world that values exploitation, people on the front lines are rarely rewarded for telling powerful senior executives that a competitive advantage is fading away. Better to shore up an existing advantage for as long as possible, until the pain becomes so obvious that there is no choice. That's what happened at IBM, Sony, Nokia, Kodak, and a host of other firms that got themselves into terrible trouble, despite ample early warnings from those working with customers.

To compete in a transient-advantage economy, you must be willing to honestly assess whether current advantages are at risk. Ask yourself which of these statements is true of your company:

- I don't buy my own company's products or services.

- We're investing at the same or higher levels and not getting better margins or growth in return.

- Customers are finding cheaper or simpler solutions to be "good enough."

- Competition is emerging from places we didn't expect.

- Customers are no longer excited about what we have to offer.

- We're not considered a top place to work by the people we'd like to hire.

- Some of our very best people are leaving.

- Our stock is perpetually undervalued.

If you nodded in agreement with four or more of these, that's a clear warning that you may be facing imminent erosion.

But it isn't enough to recognize a problem. You also have to abandon many of the traditional notions about competitive strategy that will exacerbate the challenge of strategy reinvention.

Seven Dangerous Misconceptions

Most executives working in a high-velocity setting know perfectly well that they need to change their mode of operation. Often, though, deeply embedded assumptions can lead companies into traps. Here are the ones I see most often.

The first-mover trap

This is the belief that being first to market and owning assets create a sustainable position. In some businesses—like aircraft engines or mining—that's still true. But in most industries a first-mover advantage doesn't last.

The superiority trap

Almost any early-stage technology, process, or product won't be as effective as something that's been honed and polished for years. Because of that disparity, many companies don't see the need to invest in improving their established offerings—until the upstart innovations mature, by which time it's often too late for the incumbents.

The quality trap

Many businesses in exploit mode stick with a level of quality higher than customers are prepared to pay for. When a cheaper, simpler offer is good enough, customers will abandon the incumbent.

The hostage-resources trap

In most companies, executives running big, profitable businesses get to call the shots. These people have no incentive to shift resources to new ventures. I remember holding a Nokia product that was remarkably similar to today's iPad—in about 2004. It hooked up to the internet, accessed web pages, and even had a rudimentary app constellation. Why did Nokia never capitalize on this groundbreaking innovation? Because the company's emphasis was on mass-market phones, and resource allocation decisions were made accordingly.

Is Your Company Prepared for the Transient-Advantage Economy?

To seize transient advantages, companies need a new mode of operation. The diagnostic below can help pinpoint areas where change is required. Simply position your organization's current way of working between the two statements in the assessment. If you score in the lower part of the range in an area, you might want to take a hard look at it.

Focused on extending existing advantages							Capable of coping with transient advantage
Budgets, people, and other resources are largely controlled by heads of established businesses.	1	2	3	4	5	6	7	Critical resources are controlled by a separate group that doesn't run businesses.
We tend to extend our established advantages if we can.	1	2	3	4	5	6	7	We tend to move out of an established advantage early, with the goal of moving on to something new.
We don't have a process for disengaging from a business.	1	2	3	4	5	6	7	We have a systematic way of exiting businesses.
Disengagements tend to be painful and difficult.	1	2	3	4	5	6	7	Disengagements are just part of the normal business cycle.
We try to avoid failures, even in uncertain situations.	1	2	3	4	5	6	7	We recognize that failures are unavoidable and try to learn from them.
We budget annually or for even longer.	1	2	3	4	5	6	7	We budget in quick cycles, either quarterly or on a rolling basis.

Left statement	1	2	3	4	5	6	7	Right statement
We like to stick to plans once they are formulated.	1	2	3	4	5	6	7	We are comfortable changing our plans as new information comes in.
We emphasize optimization in our approach to asset utilization.	1	2	3	4	5	6	7	We emphasize flexibility in our approach to asset utilization.
Innovation is an on-again, off-again process.	1	2	3	4	5	6	7	Innovation is an ongoing, systematic core process for us.
It's difficult for us to pull resources from a successful business to fund more uncertain opportunities.	1	2	3	4	5	6	7	It's quite normal for us to pull resources from a successful business to fund more uncertain opportunities.
Our best people spend most of their time solving problems and handling crises.	1	2	3	4	5	6	7	Our best people spend most of their time working on new opportunities for our organization.
We try to keep our organizational structure relatively stable and to fit new ideas into the existing structure.	1	2	3	4	5	6	7	We reorganize when new opportunities require a different structure.
We tend to emphasize analysis over experimentation.	1	2	3	4	5	6	7	We tend to emphasize experimentation over analysis.
It isn't easy to be candid with our senior leaders when something goes wrong.	1	2	3	4	5	6	7	We find it very easy to be candid with senior leaders when something goes wrong.

The white-space trap

When I ask executives about the biggest barriers to innovation, I often hear, "Well, these things fall between the cracks of our organizational structure." When opportunities don't fit their structure, firms often simply forgo them instead of making the effort to reorganize. For instance, a product manufacturer might pass up potentially profitable moves into services because they require coordination of activities along a customer's experience, rather than by product line.

The empire-building trap

In a lot of companies, the more assets and employees you manage, the better. This system promotes hoarding, bureaucracy building, and fierce defense of the status quo; it inhibits experimentation, iterative learning, and risk taking. And it causes employees who like to do new things to leave.

The sporadic-innovation trap

Many companies do not have a system for creating a pipeline of new advantages. As a result, innovation is an on-again, off-again process that is driven by individuals, making it extraordinarily vulnerable to swings in the business cycle.

The assessment "Is Your Company Prepared for the Transient-Advantage Economy?" will give you a sense of whether your organization is vulnerable to these traps.

Strategy for Transient Advantage: The New Playbook

Companies that want to create a portfolio of transient advantages need to make eight major shifts in the way that they operate.

1. Think about arenas, not industries

One of the more cherished ideas in traditional management is that by looking at data about other firms like yours, you can uncover the right strategy for your organization. Indeed, one of the most influential strategy frameworks, Michael Porter's five forces model, assumes that you are mainly comparing your company to others in a similar industry. In today's environment, where industry lines are quickly blurring, this can blindside you.

I've seen nontraditional competitors take companies by surprise over and over again. In the 1980s, for instance, no money-center bank even saw the threat posed by Merrill Lynch's new cash-management accounts, because they weren't offered by any bank. Millions in deposits flew out the door before the banks realized what was going on. But in recent years, the phenomenon has become more common. Google's moves into phone operating systems and online video have created consternation in traditional phone businesses; retailers like Walmart have begun edging into health care; and the entire activity of making payments is being disrupted by players from a variety of industries, including mobile phone operators, internet credit providers, and swipe-card makers.

Today strategy involves orchestrating competitive moves in what I call "arenas." An arena is a combination of a customer segment, an offer, and a place in which that offer is delivered. It isn't that industries aren't relevant anymore; it's just that industry-level analysis doesn't give you the full picture. Indeed, the very notion of a transient competitive advantage is less about making more money than your industry peers, as conventional definitions would have it, and more about responding to customers' "jobs to be done" (as Tony Ulwick would call it) in a given space.

2. Set broad themes, and
then let people experiment

The shift to a focus on arenas means that you can't analyze your way to an advantage with armies of junior staffers or consultants anymore. Today's gifted strategists examine the data, certainly, but they also use advanced pattern recognition, direct observation, and the interpretation of weak signals in the environment to set broad themes. Within those themes, they free people to try different approaches and business models. Cognizant, for instance, clearly spells out the competitive terrain it would like to claim but permits people on the ground considerable latitude within that framework. "The Future of Work" is Cognizant's umbrella term for a host of services intended to help clients rethink their business models, reinvent their workforces, and rewire their operations—all with the firm's assistance, of course.

3. Adopt metrics that support
entrepreneurial growth

When advantages come and go, conventional metrics can effectively kill off innovations by imposing decision rules that make no sense. The net present value rule, for instance, assumes that you will complete every project you start, that advantages will last for quite a while, and that there will even be a "terminal value" left once they are gone. It leads companies to underinvest in new opportunities.

Instead, firms can use the logic of "real options" to evaluate new moves. A real option is a small investment that conveys the right, but not the obligation, to make a more significant commitment in the future. It allows the organization to learn through trial and error. Consider the way Intuit has made experimentation a core strategic process, amplifying by orders of magnitude its ability to venture into new spaces and try new things. As Kaaren Hanson, the company's vice president of design innovation, said at a recent conference at Columbia Business School, the important thing is to "fall in love with the problem you are trying to solve" rather than with the solution, and to be comfortable with iteration as you work toward the answer.

4. Focus on experiences and solutions to problems

As barriers to entry tumble, product features can be copied in an instant. Even service offerings in many industries have become commoditized. Once a company has demonstrated that demand for something exists, competitors quickly move in. What customers crave—and few companies provide—are well-designed experiences and complete solutions to their problems. Unfortunately, many companies are so internally focused that they're oblivious to the customer's experience. You call up your friendly local cable company or telephone provider and get connected to a robot. The robot wants to know your customer number, which you dutifully provide. Eventually, the robot decides that your particular problem is too difficult and hands you over to a live person. What's the first thing the person wants to know? Yup, your customer number. It's symptomatic of the disjointed and fragmented way most complex organizations handle customers.

Companies skilled at exploiting transient advantage put themselves in their customers' place and consider the outcome customers are trying to achieve. Australia's Brambles has done a really great job of this even though it is in a seemingly dull industry (managing the logistics of pallets and other containers). The company realized that one of grocers' biggest costs was the labor required to shelve goods delivered to their stores. Brambles designed a solution: plastic bins that can be filled by growers right in the fields and lifted directly from pallets and placed on shelves, from which customers can help themselves. It has cut labor costs significantly. Better yet, fruits and vegetables arrive at the point of purchase in better shape because they aren't manhandled repeatedly as they go from field to box to truck to warehouse to storage room to shelf. Although seemingly low-tech, this initiative and others like it have generated substantial profits and steady growth for the company—not to mention customers' appreciation.

5. Build strong relationships and networks

One of the few barriers to entry that remain powerful in a transient-advantage context has to do with people and their personal networks. Indeed, evidence suggests that the most successful and sought-after employees are those with the most robust networks. Realizing that strong relationships with customers are a profound source of advantage, many companies have begun to invest in communities and networks as a way of deepening ties with customers. Intuit, for example, has created a space on its website where customers can interact, solve one another's problems, and share ideas. The company goes so far as to recognize exemplary problem solvers with special titles and short profiles of them on the site. Amazon and TripAdvisor both make contributions from their communities a core part of the value they offer customers. And of course, social networks have the power to enhance or destroy a firm's credibility in nanoseconds as customers enjoy an unprecedented ability to connect with one another.

Firms that are skilled at managing networks are also notable for the way they preserve important relationships. Infosys, for instance, is choosy about which customers it will serve, but it maintains a 97% customer retention rate. Sagentia, a technical consultancy in the U.K., is extremely conscientious about making sure that people who are let go remain on good terms with the firm and land well in new positions. Even at a large industrial company like GE, the senior leaders spend inordinate amounts of time building and preserving relationships with other firms.

6. Avoid brutal restructuring; learn healthy disengagement

In researching firms that effectively navigate the transient-advantage economy, I was struck by how seldom they engaged in restructuring, downsizing, or mass firings. Instead, many of them seemed to continually adjust and readjust their resources. At Infosys, I was told, people don't really believe in "chopping things off." Rather, when an initiative is wound down, they say it "finds its way to insignificance."

Sometimes, of course, downsizing or sudden shifts can't be avoided. The challenge then is disengaging from a business in the least destructive, most beneficial way. Netflix's efforts to get out of the DVD-shipping business and into streaming movies, which its management passionately believes represents the future, offer an interesting lesson in the wrong way to do this. In 2011 the company's management made two decisions that infuriated customers. It imposed a massive price increase across the board, and it split the DVD and streaming businesses into two separate organizations, which forced customers to duplicate their efforts to find and purchase movies. Let's assume that Netflix's leaders are right that eventually the DVD part of the business will shrivel up. How might the firm have exited more gracefully?

Preparing customers to transition away from old advantages is a lot like getting them to adopt a new product, but in reverse. Not all customers will be prepared to move at the same rate. There is a sequence to which customers you should transition first, second, and so on.

If, rather than raising prices for everybody, Netflix had selectively offered price discounts to those who would drop the DVD service, it would have moved that segment over to the new model. Then it could have gone to the "light user" DVD consumers and suggested that instead of getting a new DVD anytime they wanted it, they would get one once a month, say, for the same price. If they wanted the instant service, their prices would go up. That would shift another group to lower DVD usage. Then when those segments started to realize that all-streaming wasn't so bad, Netflix could have instituted the big price increase for the mainstream buyer. The point is that in trying to force many customers to move faster than they were prepared to, the company enraged them.

7. Get systematic about early-stage innovation

If advantages eventually disappear, it only makes sense to have a process for filling your pipeline with new ones. This in turn means that rather than being an on-again, off-again mishmash of projects, your innovation process needs to be carefully orchestrated.

Companies that innovate proficiently manage the process in similar ways. They have a governance structure suitable for innovation: They set aside a separate budget and staff for innovation and allow senior leaders to make go or no-go decisions about it outside the planning processes for individual businesses. The earmarked innovation budget, which gets allocated across projects, means that new initiatives don't have to compete with established businesses for resources. Such companies also have a strong sense of how innovations fit into the larger portfolio, and a line of sight to initiatives in all different stages. They hunt systematically for opportunities, usually searching beyond the boundaries of the firm and its R&D department and figuring out what customers are trying to accomplish and how the firm can help them do it.

8. Experiment, iterate, learn

As I've said for many years, a big mistake companies make all the time is planning new ventures with the same approaches they use for more-established businesses. Instead, they need to focus on experimentation and learning, and be prepared to make a shift or change emphasis as new discoveries happen. The discovery phase is followed by business model definition and incubation, in which a project takes the shape of an actual business and may begin pilot tests or serving customers. Only once the initiative is relatively stable and healthy is it ramped up. All too often, in their haste to get commercial traction, companies rush through this phase; as a result whatever product they introduce has critical flaws. They also spend way too much money before testing the critical assumptions that will spell success or failure.

Leadership as Orchestration

No leader could cognitively handle the complexity of scores of individual arenas, all at slightly different stages of development. What great leaders do is figure out some key directional guidelines, put in place good processes for core activities such as innovation, and use their influence over a few crucial inflection points to direct the flow of activities in the organization. This requires a new kind of leader—one who initiates conversations that question, rather than reinforce, the status quo. A strong leader seeks contrasting opinions and honest disagreement. Diversity increasingly becomes a tool for picking up signals that things may be changing. Broader constituencies may well become involved in the strategy process.

Finally, transient-advantage leaders recognize the need for speed. Fast and roughly right decision-making will replace deliberations that are precise but slow. In a world where advantages last for five minutes, you can blink and miss the window of opportunity. One thing about strategy hasn't changed: It still requires making tough choices about what to do and, even more important, what not to do. Even though you are orchestrating scores of arenas, you can do only so many things. So defining where you want to compete, how you intend to win, and how you are going to move from advantage to advantage is critical. While we might be tempted to throw up our hands and say that strategy is no longer useful, I think the opposite conclusion is called for. It's more important than ever. It just isn't about the status quo any longer.

Originally published in June 2013. Reprint H00MP3

Competing in the Age of AI

by Marco Iansiti and Karim R. Lakhani

I n 2019, just five years after the Ant Financial Services Group was launched, the number of consumers using its services passed the one billion mark. Spun out of Alibaba, Ant Financial uses artificial intelligence and data from Alipay—its core mobile-payments platform—to run an extraordinary variety of businesses, including consumer lending, money market funds, wealth management, health insurance, credit-rating services, and even an online game that encourages people to reduce their carbon footprint. The company serves more than 10 times as many customers as the largest U.S. banks—with less than one-tenth the number of employees. At its last round of funding, in 2018, it had a valuation of $150 billion—almost half that of JPMorgan Chase, the world's most valuable financial-services company.

Unlike traditional banks, investment institutions, and insurance companies, Ant Financial is built on a digital core. There are no workers in its "critical path" of operating activities. AI runs the show. There is no manager approving loans, no employee providing financial advice, no representative authorizing consumer medical expenses. And without the operating constraints that limit traditional firms, Ant Financial can compete in unprecedented ways and achieve unbridled growth and impact across a variety of industries.

The age of AI is being ushered in by the emergence of this new kind of firm. Ant Financial's cohort includes giants like Google, Facebook, Alibaba, and Tencent, and many smaller, rapidly growing firms, from Zebra Medical Vision and Wayfair to Indigo Ag and Ocado. Every time we use a service from one of those companies, the same remarkable thing happens: Rather than relying on traditional business processes operated by workers, managers, process engineers, supervisors, or customer service representatives, the value we get is served up by algorithms. Microsoft's CEO, Satya Nadella, refers to AI as the new "runtime" of the firm. True, managers and engineers design the AI and the software that makes the algorithms work, but after that, the system delivers value on its own, through digital automation or by leveraging an ecosystem of providers outside the firm. AI sets the prices on Amazon, recommends songs on Spotify, matches buyers and sellers on Indigo's marketplace, and qualifies borrowers for an Ant Financial loan.

The elimination of traditional constraints transforms the rules of competition. As digital networks and algorithms are woven into the fabric of firms, industries begin to function differently and the lines between them blur. The changes extend well beyond born-digital firms, as more-traditional organizations, confronted by new rivals, move toward AI-based models too. Walmart, Fidelity, Honeywell, and Comcast are now tapping

Idea in Brief

The Market Change

We're seeing the emergence of a new kind of firm—one in which artificial intelligence is the main source of value creation and delivery.

The Challenge

The AI-driven operating model is blurring the lines that used to separate industries and is upending the rules of business competition.

The Upshot

For digital startups and traditional firms alike, it's essential to understand the revolutionary impact AI has on operations, strategy, and competition.

extensively into data, algorithms, and digital networks to compete convincingly in this new era. Whether you're leading a digital startup or working to revamp a traditional enterprise, it's essential to understand the revolutionary impact AI has on operations, strategy, and competition.

The AI Factory

At the core of the new firm is a decision factory—what we call the "AI factory." Its software runs the millions of daily ad auctions at Google and Baidu. Its algorithms decide which cars offer rides on Didi, Grab, Lyft, and Uber. It sets the prices of headphones and polo shirts on Amazon and runs the robots that clean floors in some Walmart locations. It enables customer service bots at Fidelity and interprets X-rays at Zebra Medical. In each case the AI factory treats decision-making as a science. Analytics systematically convert internal and external data into predictions, insights, and choices, which in turn guide and automate operational workflows.

Oddly enough, the AI that can drive the explosive growth of a digital firm often isn't even all that sophisticated. To bring about dramatic change, AI doesn't need to be the stuff of science fiction—indistinguishable from human behavior or simulating human reasoning, a capability sometimes referred to as "strong AI." You need only a computer system to be able to perform tasks traditionally handled by people—what is often referred to as "weak AI."

With weak AI, the AI factory can already take on a range of critical decisions. In some cases it might manage information businesses (such as Google and Facebook). In other cases it will guide how the company builds, delivers, or operates actual physical products (like Amazon's warehouse robots or Waymo, Google's self-driving car service). But in all cases digital decision factories handle some of the most critical processes and operating decisions. Software makes up the core of the firm, while humans are moved to the edge.

Four components are essential to every factory. The first is the data pipeline, the semiautomated process that gathers, cleans, integrates, and safeguards data in a systematic, sustainable, and scalable way. The second is algorithms, which generate predictions about future states or actions of the business. The third is an experimentation platform, on which hypotheses regarding new algorithms are tested to ensure that their suggestions are having the intended effect. The fourth is infrastructure, the systems that embed this process in software and connect it to internal and external users.

Take a search engine like Google or Bing. As soon as someone starts to type a few letters into the search box, algorithms dynamically predict the full search term on the basis of terms that many users have typed in before and this particular user's past actions. These predictions are captured in a drop-down menu (the "autosuggest box") that helps the user zero in quickly on a relevant search. Every keystroke and every click are captured as data points, and every data point improves the predictions for future searches. AI also generates the organic search results, which are drawn from a previously assembled index of the web and optimized according to the clicks generated on the results of previous searches. The entry of the term also sets off an automated auction for the ads most relevant to the user's search, the results of which are shaped by additional experimentation and learning loops. Any click on or away from the search query or search results page provides useful data. The more searches, the better the predictions, and the better the predictions, the more the search engine is used.

Removing Limits to Scale, Scope, and Learning

The concept of scale has been central in business since at least the Industrial Revolution. The great Alfred Chandler described how modern industrial firms could reach unprecedented levels of production at much lower unit cost, giving large firms an important edge over smaller rivals. He also highlighted the benefits companies could reap from the ability to achieve greater production scope, or variety. The push for improvement and innovation added a third requirement for firms: learning. Scale, scope, and learning have come to be considered the essential drivers of a firm's operating performance. And for a long time they've been enabled by carefully defined business processes that rely on labor and management to deliver products and services to customers—and that are reinforced by traditional IT systems.

How AI-driven companies can outstrip traditional firms

The value that scale delivers eventually tapers off in traditional operating models, but in digital operating models, it can climb much higher.

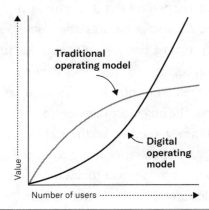

After hundreds of years of incremental improvements to the industrial model, the digital firm is now radically changing the scale, scope, and learning paradigm. AI-driven processes can be scaled up much more rapidly than traditional processes can, allow for much greater scope because they can easily be connected with other digitized businesses, and create incredibly powerful opportunities for learning and improvement—like the ability to produce ever more accurate and sophisticated customer-behavior models and then tailor services accordingly.

In traditional operating models, scale inevitably reaches a point at which it delivers diminishing returns. But we don't necessarily see this with AI-driven models, in which the return on scale can continue to climb to previously unheard-of levels. Now imagine what happens when an AI-driven firm competes with a traditional firm by serving the same customers with a similar (or better) value proposition and a much more scalable operating model.

We call this kind of confrontation a "collision." As both learning and network effects amplify volume's impact on value creation, firms built on a digital core can overwhelm traditional organizations. Consider the outcome when Amazon collides with traditional retailers, Ant Financial with traditional banks, and Didi and Uber with traditional taxi services. As Clayton Christensen, Michael Raynor, and Rory McDonald argued in "What Is Disruptive Innovation?" (HBR, December 2015), such competitive upsets don't fit the disruption model. Collisions are not caused by a particular innovation in a technology or a business model. They're the result of the emergence of a completely different kind of firm. And they can fundamentally alter industries and reshape the nature of competitive advantage.

Note that it can take quite a while for AI-driven operating models to generate economic value anywhere near the value that traditional operating models generate at scale. Network effects produce little value before they reach critical mass, and most newly applied algorithms suffer from a "cold start" before acquiring adequate data. Ant Financial grew rapidly, but its core payment service, Alipay, which had been launched in 2004 by Alibaba, took years to reach its current volume. This explains why executives ensconced in the traditional model have a difficult time at first believing that the digital model will ever catch up. But once the digital operating model really gets going, it can deliver far superior value and quickly overtake traditional firms.

Collisions between AI-driven and traditional firms are happening across industries: software, financial services, retail, telecommunications, media, health care, automobiles, and even agribusiness. It's hard to think of a business that isn't facing the pressing need to digitize its operating model and respond to the new threats.

Rebuilding Traditional Enterprises

For leaders of traditional firms, competing with digital rivals involves more than deploying enterprise software or even building data pipelines, understanding algorithms, and experimenting. It requires rearchitecting the firm's organization and operating model. For a very, very long time, companies have optimized their scale, scope, and learning through greater focus and specialization, which led to the siloed structures that the vast majority of enterprises today have. Generations of information technology didn't change this pattern. For decades, IT was used to enhance the performance of specific functions and organizational units. Traditional enterprise systems often even reinforced silos and the divisions across functions and products.

Silos, however, are the enemy of AI-powered growth. Indeed, businesses like Google Ads and Ant Financial's MyBank deliberately forgo them and are designed to leverage an integrated core of data and a unified, consistent code base. When each silo in a firm has its own data and code, internal development is fragmented, and it's nearly impossible to build connections across the silos or with external business networks or ecosystems. It's also nearly impossible to develop a 360-degree understanding of the customer that both serves and draws from every department and function. So when firms set up a new digital core, they should avoid creating deep organizational divisions within it.

While the transition to an AI-driven model is challenging, many traditional firms—some of which we've worked with—have begun to make the shift. In fact, in a recent study we looked at more than 350 traditional enterprises in both service and manufacturing sectors and found that the majority had started building a greater focus on data and analytics into their organizations.

Putting AI at the Firm's Core

The transition from a traditional firm to an AI-driven organization cannot happen in a skunkworks or be spearheaded by some separate autonomous group. It requires a holistic effort. In our research and our work with a variety of companies, we've come up with five principles that should guide transformations (beyond common best practices for leading change):

One strategy

Rearchitecting a company's operating model means rebuilding each business unit on a new, integrated foundation of data, analytics, and software. This challenging and time-consuming undertaking demands focus and a consistent top-down mandate to coordinate and inspire the many bottom-up efforts involved.

A clear architecture

A new approach based on data, analytics, and AI requires some centralization and a lot of consistency. Data assets should be integrated across a range of applications to maximize their impact. Fragmented data will be virtually impossible to safeguard consistently, especially given privacy and security considerations. If the data isn't all held in centralized repositories, then the organization must at least have an accurate catalog of where the data is, explicit guidelines for what to do with it (and how to protect it), and standards for when and how to store it so that it can be used and reused by multiple parties.

The right capabilities

Though building a base of software, data science, and advanced analytics capabilities will take time, much can be done with a small number of motivated, knowledgeable people. However, many organizations fail to realize that they need to systematically hire a very different kind of talent and set up career paths and incentive systems for those employees.

An agile "product" focus

Building an AI-centric operating model is about taking traditional processes and transforming them into software. Developing a
(continued)

Putting AI at the Firm's Core (*continued*)

product-focused mentality is essential to getting this done. Like the product managers at any world-class software development project, the IT teams deploying AI-centered applications should have a deep understanding of the use cases they're enabling—a product management orientation that goes well beyond the approach of traditional IT organizations. In the past, IT was largely about keeping old systems working, deploying software updates, protecting against cyberattacks, and running help desks. Developing operating-model software is a different game.

Multidisciplinary governance

The governance of digital assets has become increasingly important and complex and calls for well-thought-out collaboration across disparate disciplines and functions. The challenges of data privacy, algorithmic bias, and cybersecurity are increasing risk and even government intervention and regulation. Governance should integrate a legal and corporate affairs function, which may even be involved in product and technology decisions. AI requires deep thinking about legal and ethical challenges, including careful consideration of what data should be stored and preserved (and what data should not).

Many—including Nordstrom, Vodafone, Comcast, and Visa—had already made important inroads, digitizing and redesigning key components of their operating models and developing sophisticated data platforms and AI capabilities. You don't have to be a software startup to digitize critical elements of your business—but you do have to confront silos and fragmented legacy systems, add capabilities, and retool your culture. (For a closer look at the key principles that should drive such transformations, see the sidebar "Putting AI at the Firm's Core.")

Fidelity Investments is using AI to enable processes in important areas, including customer service, customer insights,

Microsoft's AI Transformation

Microsoft's transformation into an AI-driven firm took years of research but gained steam with the reorganization of its internal IT and data assets, which had been dispersed across the company's various operations. That effort was led by Kurt DelBene, the former head of Microsoft's Office business, who'd left to help fix the U.S. government's HealthCare.gov site before returning to Microsoft in 2015.

There's a reason that CEO Satya Nadella chose someone with product experience to run IT and build the "AI factory" that would be the foundation of the firm's new operating model. "Our product is the process," DelBene told us. "First, we are going to articulate what the vision should be for the systems and processes we support. Second, we're going to be run like a product development team. And we're going to be agile-based." To strengthen that orientation on his team, he brought in handpicked leaders and engineers from the product functions.

Today Core Engineering—as the IT operation is now known—is a showcase for Microsoft's own transformation. Thanks to the group's work, many traditional processes that used to be performed in silos are enabled by one consistent software base residing in Microsoft's Azure cloud. In addition, the team is driving toward a common data architecture across the company. The new, AI-based operating platform connects the sprawling organization with a shared software-component library, algorithm repository, and data catalog, all used to rapidly enable and deploy digital processes across different lines of business.

Beyond increasing productivity and scalability, the AI also helps head off problems. "We leverage AI to know when things are starting to behave in unexpected ways," DelBene says. "The best we could do in the past is react as fast as possible. Now we can preempt things, from bad contracts to cyberbreaches."

and investment recommendations. Its AI initiatives build on a multiyear effort to integrate data assets into one digital core and redesign the organization around it. The work is by no means finished, but the impact of AI is already evident in many high-value use cases across the company. To take on Amazon, Walmart is rebuilding its operating model around AI and replacing traditional siloed enterprise software systems with an integrated, cloud-based architecture. That will allow Walmart to use its unique data assets in a variety of powerful new applications and automate or enhance a growing number of operating tasks with AI and analytics. At Microsoft, Nadella is betting the company's future on a wholesale transformation of its operating model.

Rethinking Strategy and Capabilities

As AI-powered firms collide with traditional businesses, competitive advantage is increasingly defined by the ability to shape and control digital networks. (See "Why Some Platforms Thrive and Others Don't," HBR, January–February 2019.) Organizations that excel at connecting businesses, aggregating the data that flows among them, and extracting its value through analytics and AI will have the upper hand. Traditional network effects and AI-driven learning curves will reinforce each other, multiplying each other's impact. You can see this dynamic in companies such as Google, Facebook, Tencent, and Alibaba, which have become powerful "hub" firms by accumulating data through their many network connections and building the algorithms necessary to heighten competitive advantages across disparate industries.

   Meanwhile, conventional approaches to strategy that focus on traditional industry analysis are becoming increasingly ineffective. Take automotive companies. They're facing a variety of new digital threats, from Uber to Waymo, each coming from outside traditional industry boundaries. But if auto executives think of cars beyond their traditional industry context, as a highly connected, AI-enabled service, they can not only defend themselves but also unleash new value—through local commerce opportunities, ads, news and entertainment feeds, location-based services, and so on.

The advice to executives was once to stick with businesses they knew, in industries they understood. But synergies in algorithms and data flows do not respect industry boundaries. And organizations that can't leverage customers and data across those boundaries are likely to be at a big disadvantage. Instead of focusing on industry analysis and on the management of companies' internal resources, strategy needs to focus on the connections firms create across industries and the flow of data through the networks the firms use.

All this has major implications for organizations and their employees. Machine learning will transform the nature of almost every job, regardless of occupation, income level, or specialization. Undoubtedly, AI-based operating models can exact a real human toll. Several studies suggest that perhaps half of current work activities may be replaced by AI-enabled systems. We shouldn't be too surprised by that. After all, operating models have long been designed to make many tasks predictable and repeatable. Processes for scanning products at checkout, making lattes, and removing hernias, for instance, benefit from standardization and don't require too much human creativity. While AI improvements will enrich many jobs and generate a variety of interesting opportunities, it seems inevitable that they will also cause widespread dislocation in many occupations.

The dislocations will include not only job replacement but also the erosion of traditional capabilities. In almost every setting, AI-powered firms are taking on highly specialized organizations. In an AI-driven world, the requirements for competition have less to do with specialization and more to do with a universal set of capabilities in data sourcing, processing, analytics, and algorithm development. These new universal capabilities are reshaping strategy, business design, and even leadership. Strategies in very diverse digital and networked businesses now look similar, as do the drivers of operating performance. Industry expertise has become less critical. When Uber looked for a new CEO, the board hired someone who had previously run a digital firm—Expedia—not a limousine services company.

We're moving from an era of core competencies that differ from industry to industry to an age shaped by data and analytics and powered by algorithms—all hosted in the cloud for anyone to use. This is why Alibaba and Amazon are able to compete in industries as disparate as retail and financial services, and health care and credit scoring. These sectors now have many similar technological foundations and employ common methods and tools. Strategies are shifting away from traditional differentiation based on cost, quality, and brand equity and specialized, vertical expertise and toward advantages like business network position, the accumulation of unique data, and the deployment of sophisticated analytics.

The Leadership Challenge

Though it can unleash enormous growth, the removal of operating constraints isn't always a good thing. Frictionless systems are prone to instability and hard to stop once they're in motion.

Think of a car without brakes or a skier who can't slow down. A digital signal—a viral meme, for instance—can spread rapidly through networks and can be just about impossible to halt, even for the organization that launched it in the first place or an entity that controls the key hubs in a network. Without friction, a video inciting violence or a phony or manipulative headline can quickly spread to billions of people on a variety of networks, even morphing to optimize click-throughs and downloads. If you have a message to send, AI offers a fantastic way to reach vast numbers of people and personalize that message for them. But the marketer's paradise can be a citizen's nightmare.

Digital operating models can aggregate harm along with value. Even when the intent is positive, the potential downside can be significant. A mistake can expose a large digital network to a destructive cyberattack. Algorithms, if left unchecked, can exacerbate bias and misinformation on a massive scale. Risks can be greatly magnified. Consider the way that digital banks are aggregating consumer savings in an unprecedented fashion. Ant Financial, which now operates one of the largest money market funds in the world, is entrusted with the savings of hundreds of millions of Chinese consumers. The risks that presents are significant, especially for a relatively unproven institution.

Digital scale, scope, and learning create a slew of new challenges—not just privacy and cybersecurity problems, but social turbulence resulting from market concentration, dislocations, and increased inequality. The institutions designed to keep an eye on business—regulatory bodies, for example—are struggling to keep up with all the rapid change.

In an AI-driven world, once an offering's fit with a market is ensured, user numbers, engagement, and revenues can skyrocket. Yet it's increasingly obvious that unconstrained growth is dangerous. The potential for businesses that embrace digital operating models is huge, but the capacity to inflict widespread harm needs to be explicitly considered. Navigating these opportunities and threats will be a real test of leadership for both businesses and public institutions.

Originally published in January–February 2020. Reprint R1306C

6

In the Ecosystem Economy, What's Your Strategy?

by Michael G. Jacobides

W hen Nestlé was preparing to go mainstream with Nespresso, its single-use espresso capsule, it knew that users would need a machine specifically designed to work with the pod. So the company cultivated a network of manufacturers. It didn't tell customers to buy a Jura, a Krups, or a Braun—it just decided which manufacturers could be on the list. And because the capsule and its interface were patented, other manufacturers could not make Nespresso-compatible machines without permission.

Nespresso was creating—designing—an ecosystem: an orchestrated network spanning multiple sectors. The firms involved work to shared standards, sometimes on a shared platform, to make their products and services compatible. And they create links among themselves that make it difficult for outsiders to break in.

Designed ecosystems like Nespresso's are increasingly important, owing to the convergence of three big structural changes in our economy. The first is an unprecedented rollback of regulations protecting firms that once had the exclusive privilege of serving particular customer needs. As those protections fall, organizations in other domains are free to partner to provide more-integrated offerings, as when accountancies team up with law firms. The second change is a blurring of the separation between products and services because of regulatory changes and digitization. The latter has also led to offerings with more-modular structures whose components can be recombined in new ways, which in turn has encouraged the rise of product-service bundles provided by networks of interdependent suppliers. The third change involves technology that is revolutionizing how firms can serve their customers. Our dependence on mobile devices, along with the internet's influence on buying patterns, has dramatically expanded the possibilities for linking previously unrelated goods and services—reinforcing the effects of the first two changes.

Given these shifts, it is less and less likely that single firms can offer all the elements a customer needs—let alone afford to experiment with them. And so ecosystems, especially designed ones, are on the rise. In fact, in a growing number of sectors the firm and even the industry have ceased to be meaningful units of strategic analysis. We must focus instead on competition between digitally enabled designed ecosystems that span traditional industry boundaries and offer complex and customizable product-service bundles.

Traditional strategy frameworks are of little help when designing or participating in such an ecosystem. An ecosystem-focused framework, as opposed to a firm-focused one, needs to answer five questions.

Idea in Brief

The Challenge

In an increasing number of contexts, the firm is no longer an independent strategic actor. Its success depends on collaboration with other firms in an ecosystem spanning multiple sectors.

Why It Arose

The growing importance of ecosystems is linked to the convergence of three big structural changes: a rollback of regulatory protections, a blurring of the separation between products and services, and technology that revolutionizes how firms can serve customers.

How to Meet It

An ecosystem-focused framework can help managers answer five key questions: Can you help other firms create value? What role should you play? What should the terms be? Can your organization adapt? How many ecosystems should you manage?

1. Can You Help Other Firms Create Value?

In ecosystem competition, success is as much about helping other firms innovate as it is about being innovative yourself. Companies that have built a successful ecosystem have often done so incrementally, broadening the value proposition of their core offering by finding opportunities to apply one of its features or functionalities to some previously unrelated product or service.

Consider Google's Nest, which started by developing a smart digital thermostat that can be controlled remotely. It then added an alarm, thus building a bundle that controls both comfort and security. Next, capitalizing on the possibilities of digital interconnections, it created the Works with Nest ecosystem, which lets firms innovate by connecting with Nest. For instance, LIFX designed a Nest-compatible system whereby red LEDs flash if the smoke or safety alarms are activated—a literal lifesaver for the hard of hearing. Fitbit, the wearable fitness tracker, can tell Nest you're awake so that it knows to warm your home. And Mercedes-Benz cars can use GPS to tell Nest to switch on the heat as you arrive. These extensions constitute a value proposition greater than anything Nest could have provided on its own. (Google recently announced that it will be phasing out Works with Nest and transitioning to Works with Google Assistant—an even broader and stronger ecosystem.)

That proposition rests on shared functionality. Nest may have started as a remotely controllable thermostat, but its creators realized that consumers might want to remotely control multiple services and products in multiple contexts. That understanding pointed the way to possible complementors, and Nest gradually migrated to providing remote control for a range of home systems and appliances.

Having identified a critical and shareable functionality, an ecosystem builder needs to consider the incentives and motivations of potential complementors. How will joining your ecosystem look from their point of view? Will they be content to remain complementors, or could they reasonably hope to compete with you? In Nest's case, what value proposition could it offer Mercedes—that is, how could participation improve the way Mercedes embeds itself in its customers' daily lives? How did that compare with other options Mercedes had?

If you don't focus on the needs of your partners, your ecosystem will wither on the vine, no matter how strong your brand and market position; chances are that some other ecosystem builder can offer a better alternative. Nokia's downfall provides a cautionary example. Even though the firm's Symbian operating system started out as the de facto ruler of the mobile telephony space, it was soon eclipsed because Nokia focused on its own narrow needs. Treated as dispensable supply-chain subordinates, app developers and other complementors jumped ship to Android.

2. What Role Should You Play?

Many firms assume they should be the focus and chief architect of any ecosystem they create. That's not necessarily the case; sometimes you are better off sharing the role or being a complementor.

To be the orchestrator and prime mover of an ecosystem, you need a superior product or service that is hard to replicate. This means some combination of IP protection, a large network of users, and strong branding. Nespresso, as mentioned, patented its capsule. The apps powering Uber and Facebook are so user-friendly that those companies very quickly built large user networks. And Apple's patent protection and user base are bolstered by a strong brand and large scale, positioning the company to orchestrate pretty much any ecosystem in which it participates.

Organizational and cultural factors are also critical. Few would disagree that orchestrators need the agility to respond to new challengers, the humility to understand customer needs, and the vision to inspire complementors. But to say that isn't necessarily to state the obvious; consider the impact a single-minded focus on shareholder value and cost control can have on a company's ability to demonstrate those qualities. Firms with that focus are often, and sometimes rightly, accused of favoring the capture of short-term profits over the creation of long-term value—and given the time needed to shape an ecosystem's parts into a successful whole, that orientation could compromise a firm's ability to be an effective orchestrator. A company whose identity is deeply rooted in its technology or management system might also struggle. For example, an obsession with control could get in the way of engaging with entrepreneurial scientists, while a preference for organic, internally generated growth could lead to clashes with complementors equally protective of their turf.

If you lack the qualifications to build an ecosystem but have an IP-protected product or service that could anchor one, your best bet most likely involves attracting the interest of a large company that could buy into or license your idea. If a small-scale HVAC installer had come up with a remotely controllable thermostat, it probably could not have attracted the ecosystem of complementors that Google did. But it could have approached Google with the idea and served as a complementor while benefiting from licensing revenue. For many medium-size firms, a key strategy is to embed in many ecosystems. LIFX, for instance, connects with customers through Amazon's Alexa, Google Home, and Apple HomeKit.

Even if you bring a great product or service to the party and have the organizational and cultural capabilities to attract complementors, it might make sense to orchestrate in partnership with another firm in order to reach critical mass. Daimler and BMW recently announced plans to jointly create a managed-mobility ecosystem combining car sharing, ride hailing, parking, and other services. Concerned about disruption from firms such as Uber and Lyft, the automakers decided to collaborate on high-end services anchored to their brands—their chief differentiator and element of value, which a wholesale migration to mobility-as-a-service (MaaS) might well erode.

A big company can also buy into an ecosystem, which can be particularly helpful if its contribution is interchangeable with other firms' offerings. Toyota recently invested $1.5 billion in the Southeast Asian ride-hailing company Grab, reasoning that MaaS will drive demand for reliable low-cost cars. That partnership, the company hopes, will give Toyota not just a direct edge as a car supplier but also an understanding of car usage patterns that could confer an advantage over rivals such as Hyundai and Nissan.

Some notes of caution for mainstream firms: Even if you are large, you may be vulnerable to disruption from Google, Apple, or other tech giants, and participating in one of their ecosystems as a complementor may have significant advantages over trying to orchestrate your own—especially when it's hard to assess what combination of products and services will satisfy the final customer, or when the range of potential combinations is very broad. You should probably not be responsible for entrepreneurial and creative inputs; in the video game industry, for example, developers organize flexibly through video game engines to take their offerings to consumers. And even if you ultimately want to build your own ecosystem, participating in another one can help you gain experience, understand the needs of customers and complementors, and build the skills that orchestrating requires.

3. What Should the Terms for Participation Be?

Research on ecosystem governance is still in its early days. But governance failures are easy to identify. For instance, as described earlier, Symbian failed in part because Nokia neglected to take other parties' interests into account. Contrast that with Apple's record with app developers.

There are two key governance choices.

Access

Early in the process an ecosystem builder needs to decide whether the system should be *open, managed,* or *closed.* In an open ecosystem (such as Uber's drivers), complementors need only meet certain basic standards to participate. In a managed ecosystem (such as Apple's App Store), there are clear criteria for complementors and possibly some limits on their number, along with specific guidelines—on functionality and pricing, say. In a closed ecosystem (such as VW's connected cars and Philips's digital health), approval of complementors and rules of participation are tightly controlled.

In general, the more open the system, the easier it is to attract complementors and a wide range of products—but quality is more variable. The degree of openness should be determined in part by what matters most to the final customer. For a mobile app platform with a diverse customer base, for example, an open ecosystem—one offering lots of choice—might make sense. But if quality and safety concerns arise, barriers may be in order. Think of DiDi, China's largest ride-hailing company. Reeling from the 2018 murders of two passengers by drivers for its Hitch service, the firm chose to become more closed; it suspended Hitch and now rigorously vets prospective DiDi drivers.

Attachment

As you determine how accessible to make your ecosystem, you'll also need to consider how exclusively attached to it you want your complementors to be—how much they need to cospecialize with you. There will be trade-offs for all parties. If your mobile operating system forbids app developers from porting their programs to other platforms, the developers will certainly have a stake in your success. But the restriction might cause them not to join if they have opportunities elsewhere. Conversely, if you impose no barriers to redeploying an app, you'll find it far easier to recruit complementors, but they will have no particular attachment to your ecosystem.

The degree to which an orchestrator can lock in complementors generally depends on the attractiveness of that orchestrator and what alternatives are available. A hugely attractive orchestrator such as Apple, which can link an app developer to a large and loyal network, can probably require more attachment than a new entrant can. Compared with Apple, Android was easy to join; Google wanted it to gain traction before scaling up. Symbian ignored its developers' increasing alternatives and collapsed when those developers decamped to Apple and Google.

Their power and attractiveness, along with a lack of alternatives, have historically given tech giants such as Apple and Google relatively free rein to aggressively manage access and attachment to their ecosystems. But as technologies and attitudes change, less hierarchical ecosystems are growing more popular. WeWork's meteoric rise resulted from the fact that it not only provides shared office space but also builds communities: The WeWork app allows members to collaborate with and provide services to one another with little interference. Not-for-profits, too, are setting up nonhierarchical ecosystems; one example is the Ellen MacArthur Foundation's CE100 network, which supports firms that promote the so-called circular economy. Some smaller ventures have gone in a similar direction: The London-based platform upstart Common Objective matches up companies in the fashion industry without imposing its own "rules of the game."

More radically, the rapid growth of ledger technologies such as blockchain opens up new possibilities for creating sets of interconnected companies. The members of these ecosystems are linked not through a hub firm but through a distributed system—designed by one company, perhaps, but used by many. Consider Blanc Labs' Nekso, the biggest challenger to Uber in Mexico City. Instead of assembling a fleet of individual drivers who connect with customers through an app (the Uber model), it built an interface that allows taxi companies to band together in a network passengers can choose from, providing the same seamless experience Uber offers but through a decentralized ecosystem.

4. Can Your Organization Adapt?

An ecosystem's members must be able to quickly adapt, because the needs of the final customer, along with the desire and ability of complementors to collaborate, can shift dramatically.

Take Nike's FuelBand, an early fitness tracker that connected with other Nike products. After the arrival of Fitbit and other competing products, Nike discontinued production; the market could easily serve the need it had met, diminishing the value-add of a tracker tied to its own brand. The company also failed to defend its software and became a third-party app, salvaging what it could through a deal to codevelop a version of the Apple Watch. Like many other traditional, vertically integrated firms, Nike was slow to recognize the inevitable, and thus it lost its chance to orchestrate the wearables ecosystem.

Apple's success with the iPhone, in contrast, was fueled by the company's recognition, in 2008, that its original strategy of providing all the phone's apps was wrong. Steve Jobs—who was initially opposed to non-Apple app providers—made an impressive U-turn, creating the iPhone App Store. This both allowed the firm to share revenue from apps sold and encouraged others to find ways to leverage the phone.

Participating in an ecosystem requires an outward-facing culture and the ability to manage relationships with a host of complementors. Those skills don't come easily to established players, which tend to default to one of two approaches: to create a vertically integrated, tightly controlled network, as Nokia did, or to hop on the bandwagon of open innovation and production, providing only a platform and leaving ecosystem management up to users. The risk there is that without some central impetus or incentive from the host, other parties may fail to engage. That happened with Watson, IBM's AI developer platform: Initial developer enthusiasm did not translate into activity and engagement.

There really aren't any default strategies for building an ecosystem. You need to decide carefully where and how to open up and then do so in a way that fits your competitive environment. Nest got this right: Concerned that by opening up the alarm function it would compromise its ability to control the home, it made a strategic decision to engage in alarm and monitoring itself rather than link up with Alarm.com or Honeywell. It invited complementors in other, nonstrategic areas instead. For its part, when Alarm.com entered the thermostat market, it chose to enable Nest connectivity; having a smaller installed base and less muscle than Google, it placed a premium on the ability to infiltrate more houses, more effectively, even if that reduced its aspirations for control.

Moving beyond strategy, to build an ecosystem you will need to manage your organization. The old part of it—that which currently generates revenue—will want to keep innovation under the firm's control and will treat complementors with suspicion, whereas the new parts will need to be externally focused.

Big firms often separate the two parts, regarding the core as a margin-preserving inertial supertanker and hoping that a small fleet of "speedboats," some of which manage ecosystems, will pull the firm forward. Banks and insurance companies, for instance, often try to preserve their legacy structures and IT systems, hoping that a few add-ons will bring them into the digital, ecosystem-enabled age. But to succeed, ecosystems must be more closely aligned with the core.

New organizational structures are emerging that are better suited than traditional ones to handle these challenges. One example is the Chinese manufacturer Haier's *rendanheyi* model. Haier is organized around independently managed "microenterprises" that it may or may not own. IT facilitates information and data flows across the microenterprise units, each of which becomes, in a sense, an internal ecosystem with relatively porous boundaries, enabling the firm as a whole to position itself in a broader ecosystem.

5. How Many Ecosystems Should You Manage?

Some successful orchestrators manage a number of synergistic ecosystems, each covering a different part of the business and leading to a different path for expansion.

The Chinese tech giant Alibaba grew by creating an expanding set of connected ecosystems, starting in one market and shifting to others as it capitalized on customer information and refined its understanding of customer needs. It began with 1688.com (a wholesale marketplace), created Taobao (a C2C marketplace), moved into TMall (a third-party-seller B2C ecosystem), and expanded to Juhuasuan (a sales and marketing platform). And it is a part owner of Ant Financial, the world's most valuable fintech firm, which aims "to expand its ecosystem by penetrating more consumption scenarios in daily life."

The most obvious consequence of this dynamic is the growing dominance of national e-commerce and e-services by a small number of firms. In China, the almost equally huge Tencent and Baidu compete with Alibaba, which in many ways they resemble. Their Western equivalents are Google, Apple, Facebook, Amazon, and Microsoft. Aspiring to provide a unified service, these companies are shifting into ever more sectors, often through interfaces such as voice-activated assistants that appear seamless to the consumer. Mobility firms are doing similar things. Uber's expansion—think of Uber Eats and all the ventures of Uber Everything—demonstrates the company's ambition to integrate multiple ecosystems and manage the customer interface. Southeast Asian mobility firms such as Grab (Singapore) and Go-Jek (Indonesia) have gotten into payments as well, aiming to make themselves indispensable to the final customer.

As Marco Iansiti and Karim Lakhani recently noted, such hub firms are becoming formidable strategic bottlenecks that can direct the lion's share of value to themselves. But although it may seem that the future belongs to big, established firms with deep pockets and technological prowess, smaller upstarts (like Alibaba when it started, less than 20 years ago) and nontechnology firms have the potential to muscle in. The Chinese insurance and financial services conglomerate Ping An began by becoming more technologically savvy and soon ventured into adjacent areas, starting with health care and extending to lifestyle, in the process becoming the world's most valuable insurance group. It did so by creating focused ecosystems such as Ping An Good Doctor, which combines AI with physicians to provide medical advice, and Ping An Haofang, the country's largest online property platform. It has invested in Autohome, China's largest used-car marketplace, and in entertainment, through an alliance with Huayi Brothers. It then combined those verticals with some of its own units, including Ping An Bank and Zhong An insurance, to create the PingOne account: an offering that seeks to capture every customer interaction.

For complementors, different ecosystems represent different pathways to market—and most integrators are complementors in rivals' ecosystems (you'll find Microsoft Word in Android, Google Maps in Apple, Apple software in Microsoft systems, and so on). Firms choose to "multihome" according to what specific ecosystems allow, the cost of redeploying in other ecosystems, and the benefits of cross-ecosystem customer reach.

A firm's role in one ecosystem may drive its participation in (or orchestration of) another, and there is plenty of room for strategizing. Samsung, the biggest user of the Android ecosystem—it sells more than 40% of Android phones—threatened to create a rival OS ecosystem if Google didn't make certain concessions. The companies reached a compromise, but they continue to compete over functions such as digital assistants, and the boundaries between Google's and Samsung's phone ecosystems continue to be hotly contested. Strategic interactions of this kind between firms and their associated ecosystems will only increase.

From Private Benefit to Public Good

The rise of ecosystem-based competition not only requires a new strategic framework and organizational model; it has significant implications for policy and regulation. In particular, the increasing success of integrators and their ability to become all-powerful orchestrators across an ever-growing number of ecosystems raises serious questions about a new form of market power.

Governments must strike a balance that both keeps their business environments healthy and safeguards their societies. Little global consensus has emerged about where that balance should lie. The rapid growth of many Chinese firms has relied on their unfettered ability to access data, while Europe sets tight restrictions on that activity. Will those limit economic growth in Europe relative to China? Maybe, but Europeans may consider the price worth paying, given the social benefits of privacy protections.

Whatever social priorities they set, all countries will need to change the analytical foundations of competition law, which has long focused on managing the market shares of individual firms. As a recent report prepared for the U.K. Treasury argued, we need to adjust our approach to competition and regulation. In particular, we need to examine the terms of engagement in ecosystems, how orchestrators and integrators exert their power, what customer data those parties own, and how they interact with complementors. And while there is only one Apple, there are 2 million app developers. The fate of complementors may have more far-reaching societal effects than the high-profile fortunes of an orchestrator will have, and as we contemplate regulatory action, we must consider ecosystem governance, rules of engagement, and the well-being of the myriad, de facto weaker, complementors. We must also ask whether firms' desire to expand their reach and control an increasingly broad swath of activity restricts competition. To that end, the M&A of ecosystem plays should be scrutinized.

In approaching these challenges, policymakers should avoid the trap of treating all emerging ecosystems as commercial monsters in need of control. Ecosystems can provide new ways of bridging private benefit and public good. IDEO's CoLab circular economy portfolio advises firms in the textile and food sectors on reconfiguring their ecosystems to encourage the reuse of resources and the reduction of waste. Traipse's My Local Token provides localized digital currencies for U.S. downtowns that reinforce connections between residents and tourists on one hand and local businesses on the other. Velocia is creating a rewards ecosystem that encourages the use of public transit alongside on-demand services such as carpooling and carsharing to improve people's commutes. (Disclosure: I have advised all three of these companies.)

. . .

Business is undergoing a paradigm shift as a result of digital innovation: The very nature of competition is changing. Competing is increasingly about identifying new ways to collaborate and connect rather than simply offering alternative value propositions. But as the scope of opportunity expands, so too does the confusion of executives confronted with digital ecosystems. The complexity of those systems doesn't mean we should give up trying to make sense of them; it means we need to adjust. We must shift from rigid strategies based on prescriptive frameworks to dynamic experiments based on a process of inquiry. Start by asking yourself the five questions I've just proposed.

Originally published in September–October 2019. Reprint R1905J

Why Isn't Your Strategy Sticking?

by Andrea Belk Olson

I n 1992, Robert Kaplan and David Norton identified four barriers to effective strategy implementation: lack of understanding, lack of communication, disconnected incentives, and disconnected budgets. Over the decades, other experts have expanded on this list, identifying additional barriers including unaligned goals, insufficient resources, and inadequate performance tracking. Yet successful strategy implementation is still an ongoing struggle today. Are leaders simply not communicating well enough? Or does the intrinsic problem lie elsewhere?

The true problem lies not with the tactical aspects of strategy implementation but with psychological ones. When leaders think about the mindset needed to enact successful change, they need to first examine what will help shape perceptions. That is, they need to adopt a *contextual mindset* rather than an operational one—a mindset that looks at the entire organizational landscape and identifies the soft, hidden barriers that impede progress.

Here's how to shift from an operational to a contextual mindset so that you can better identify the hidden obstacles that may thwart your own strategy's implementation—and address them before they take root.

Understand the environment in which the strategy will live and operate

Strategy does not exist in a bubble, and the environment in which it operates influences the organization's acceptance of it.

Here's an example from one of our clients. After months of work behind closed doors, they launched a new corporate strategy. The announcement was met with reticence, doubt, and trepidation. This was due not only to a lack of communication but also to the organizational environment. For decades, the company had sustained a very rigid and hierarchical operation. Individual departments had little to no autonomy in decision-making—even the smallest decisions had to be approved in advance by a steering committee. So when the new strategy was announced, everyone adopted a "wait and see" mentality and sat tight for explicit direction from leadership rather than acting on the new program. There was no excitement about it, no buy-in.

To explore your own organizational context and identify potential strategy impediments, review your existing policies, procedures, and organizational structure. What creates barriers to action and decision-making for employees? What would create confusion or cause second-guessing?

Understand the cognitive obstacles

Any organizational pain from previous strategies is never fully forgotten. This is referred to as "historical baggage"—past experiences, perceptions, and attitudes that influence the acceptance

Idea in Brief

The Challenge

Despite careful planning and execution, many organizations struggle to implement strategies that endure over time, leading to frustration and wasted resources.

The Solution

To ensure that strategies stick, leaders must focus on aligning them with the organization's culture, capabilities, and incentives, as well as on clearly communicating them to employees. They should also work to understand the hidden obstacles that can derail a strategy's success, including the environment in which it will operate, organizational pain from past stalled strategies, and employees' unspoken doubts about the new plan.

The Payoff

Executives who recognize and address the historical context that influences employee behaviors and mindsets can build legitimacy and shift perceptions about the strategic direction.

of change. In fact, these cognitive obstacles can stall implementation before a new strategy is even introduced.

Another one of our clients recently developed a new corporate strategy. Their department leaders were tasked with getting their teams up to speed, building excitement, and providing implementation guidance for their areas. However, this strategy was the fifth iteration in two years. Employees saw it as simply a fly-by-night plan. They already believed it would be no different than the unsuccessful strategies that came before it. People resisted buy-in for fear of investing effort into something that would change again in a matter of months.

This is another reason you need to examine your own company's relationship with strategy—determining what has occurred in the past, the results of those efforts, and collective sentiment.

Use a simple combination of surveys and qualitative interviews with managers and staff. What are people's past experiences with strategy implementation? What has caused issues before, and why did those problems occur?

Address the unspoken doubts and elephants in the room

Once you have established a lay of the land, identify those concerns that come up again and again. Even if they seem illogical or petty, it is essential to proactively address these psychological barriers in a salient way, prior to beginning your strategy implementation. The key is to recognize the issues, give them legitimacy, and provide clear reasoning and solutions.

Going back to our previous example, why would this latest version of an ever-changing strategy be different? First, openly admit what occurred in the past. Second, provide real-life instances and examples that validate the concern and show it is fully understood. Third, illustrate key differences that confirm and authenticate a change in the current context. In this case, the entrance of a new competitor, along with changes in key executive personnel, were the catalysts for a renewed strategy commitment.

Follow through with necessary change

All of this will be perceived as lip service if your hidden barriers aren't genuinely addressed. However, some barriers may be more complicated to fix than others. For example, say that through your examination a specific person in the company is mentioned who has consistently derailed progress in the past. Depending on the individual and their role, there may be limitations in moving them or removing them. But this doesn't mean you ignore the problem and hope employees don't notice.

You may need time to determine a permanent solution, which might require multiple discussions, meetings, trainings, or the hiring of additional personnel. Rather than sustaining radio silence with employees until the situation is fully handled, provide a short-term stopgap. This could be something as simple as changing an approval process or shifting a person's responsibilities temporarily.

. . .

It's insufficient to simply share the goals and objectives of your strategy and hope implementation will succeed. Instead, focus on recognizing and addressing the historical context that influences employee behaviors and mindsets. That way, leaders can build legitimacy and shift perceptions by eliminating hidden mental barriers—clearing the way for strategy implementation to take flight.

Adapted from hbr.org, March 27, 2024. Reprint H083FX

How to Avoid the Agility Trap

by Jianwen Liao and Feng Zhu

Suning, once a market leader in China's retail sector, was a poster child for agile strategy. While many traditional retailers hesitated in responding to new technologies and evolving consumer preferences, Suning repeatedly pounced on digital trends and other opportunities.

In 2009, Suning embraced e-commerce, pioneering an integrated online-offline retail approach. In 2012 it began to expand its market presence significantly, moving into multiple sectors beyond its base in appliances in order to compete with e-commerce giants. One of its first acquisitions was Redbaby, a leading online seller of maternal and baby products. Setting the ambitious goal of becoming "Walmart + Amazon," the company planned to establish more than 300 Suning.com Stores and 50 Suning Plazas by 2020.

Meanwhile, video streaming was taking off in China, attracting major players like Baidu, which launched iQiyi in 2010 and later integrated it with another service, PPS, which it acquired for $370 million in 2013. Suning quickly responded, investing $250 million in PPTV, a competitor to PPS, jumping into the market even before Alibaba did. In 2015, inspired by Alibaba's launch of its financial arm, the Ant Group, Suning introduced a financial division, Suning Finance, and in 2017 it established a digital bank. About the same time, the company also entered the sports industry, investing in Jiangsu Football Club and acquiring a majority share in Inter Milan Football Club. In 2019, copying Alibaba's introduction of an omnichannel retail approach, Suning bought Wanda Department Stores and took a stake in Carrefour China, with the aim of becoming an omnichannel retailer too. In sum, Suning set out to aggressively diversify its business model while integrating its retail operations with businesses in various complementary sectors, extending its market reach, increasing its data-gathering capabilities, and enhancing customer engagement.

But its continually evolving strategy did not enable the company to thrive. In the face of sustained losses, Suning had to begin withdrawing from noncore retail ventures in 2021, aiming to streamline operations. It now confronts a challenging path to regaining market leadership.

Suning's experience is a wake-up call for the many companies that proactively adapt to market shifts. The firm displayed remarkable agility by continually responding to changes in the business landscape and seizing new opportunities—and in doing so, was following the conventional wisdom of numerous scholars and industry experts. However, as our study of many firms shows, that wisdom is faulty. We have repeatedly found that in a highly volatile environment, firms anchoring their strategies in enduring factors, rather than transient ones, are

Idea in Brief

The Problem

Companies that try to respond to every market shift often find that their performance plunges—and have to sell off their "strategic" investments at a loss.

Why It Happens

The landscape is evolving so rapidly today that companies can't keep up with every change. Attempts to do so weaken the focus on existing competitive advantages, foster a short-term strategic mindset, and create serious organizational problems.

The Solution

Build your strategies not on what changes but on what remains constant, such as customers' most fundamental needs. Begin by identifying a desired end state, what will be required to achieve it, and the enduring forces in your industry. Then match your capabilities to those constants and anchor any adaptations in them.

more likely to achieve sustainable growth. We call this approach *strategic constancy,* and we believe that companies that practice it often turn out to be more resilient in times of adversity than companies that aggressively practice agility.

The Problem with Agility

Let's begin by revisiting the assumptions underlying the theory that agility is always good for a firm's strategy.

Agility—the ability to quickly react to rapid change—is all the rage in strategy circles these days. Its popularity is rooted in the belief that organizations must constantly respond to technological advances, new market dynamics, shifting consumer preferences, and other external developments. That sounds like a sensible proposition, but in practice continual strategic adaptation is almost impossible to pull off, because the business environment is evolving so fast that firms can't keep up. The consequences for those that try to are stark:

Erosion of competitive advantages

Attempting to adapt to every perceived shift or threat can spread organizational resources thin and weaken the focus on core competencies. Building a competitive advantage is a gradual process and often requires concentrating on a select group of synergistic activities over a long period. Suning took just the opposite tack: Its overemphasis on adaptation led it to diversify too much. Many of its new ventures shared few synergies, and it didn't have enough time to establish a competitive foothold in new sectors before transitioning to other opportunities.

Strategic myopia

A preoccupation with adaptation can foster a short-term focus. When change is swift and numerous opportunities arise at once, companies driven by an agility mindset may chase them all simultaneously and succumb to the temptation to lean hardest into the ones that offer the quickest returns. Firms may overlook the need for coherence in the business portfolio and search constantly for the next big thing. As a result they may neglect to develop the vision and long-term capabilities they need to achieve sustained success.

Organizational chaos

When a company changes direction, it's imperative that the operating model—the organization's structure, processes, personnel, and culture—be realigned with the new goals. The company needs to prepare for the transition, oversee it, and then solidify the new operating model to ensure that it lasts. Implementing such organizational realignments is time-consuming. If they're continual, they can exhaust employees, damaging morale and productivity and undermining transformation initiatives. The incessant flux of the external environment can also overwhelm managers, leading them to make hasty, poorly thought-out decisions. If companies are perpetually adjusting their operating models in response to environmental fluctuations, they risk descending into organizational chaos.

So what can firms do to avoid these problems?

Embracing Strategic Constancy

Jeff Bezos, the founder of Amazon, once made an interesting observation: "I very frequently get the question: 'What's going to change in the next 10 years?' . . . I almost never get the question: 'What's not going to change in the next 10 years?' And I submit to you that that second question is actually the more important of the two—because you can build a business strategy around the things that are stable in time."

He continued: "In our retail business, we know that customers want low prices, and I know that's going to be true 10 years from now. They want fast delivery; they want vast selection. It's impossible to imagine a future 10 years from now where a customer comes up and says, 'Jeff, I love Amazon; I just wish the prices were a little higher,' or 'I love Amazon; I just wish you'd deliver a little more slowly.' Impossible."

Bezos's philosophy underscores the importance of understanding and catering to fundamental consumer needs that are consistent over time, rather than getting caught up in the transient trends that businesses often chase. By focusing on the strategic constants, Amazon can confidently invest in infrastructure, technology, and processes that cater to unchanging customer desires, ensuring that any investment made today will continue to contribute to the company's success for many years to come.

This is a classic example of strategic constancy, which requires a firm to maintain a steadfast focus on a long-term vision even as it navigates a dynamic business environment. It's about recognizing the enduring aspects of a company's business model— its core values, customer relationships, brand identity, and key competencies—and remaining committed to them despite external pressures. It emphasizes depth over breadth—deepening the company's competitive advantage in its core areas rather than spreading efforts over many. Because it ensures continuity in an organization's vision, it also facilitates more-reliable strategic planning and execution.

Strategic constants are few in number. In the retail industry, for example, they might be cost, efficiency, and customer experience. In auto manufacturing, they might be safety, reliability, and design.

Some strategic constants may seem intuitive—online platforms like Amazon will always need efficient fulfillment—but others may be less obvious and require firms to make hard choices. For example, fast-fashion companies such as Zara, H&M, and Shein must figure out whether affordability and trendiness will continue to be the driving forces of their industry amid the growing awareness of sustainability issues.

In contrast to strategic constants, transient factors are abundant, stemming from fluctuating and often unpredictable market trends, regulatory shifts, and technological changes. In retail, transient factors could include evolving formats, like big-box stores, and new e-commerce models, such as group buying, social-media-based sales, content commerce, and internet-of-things transactions. In auto manufacturing, transient factors might include new design trends, supply chain disruptions, fluctuations in interest rates, chip shortages, and government subsidies. The impact of transient factors is temporary, and their low predictability creates challenges for strategic planning. Understanding these distinctions is crucial for businesses.

Costco, a retailer established well before the digital era, epitomizes strategic constancy with its dedication to supply chain excellence. It limits its product offerings to about 4,000 SKUs, which enables it to buy products in bulk so that it can always offer deep price discounts to fee-paying members. That model ensures that it has a strong competitive position, regardless of the changing landscape.

Creating a Strategically Constant Company

Let's turn now to how to use a focus on strategic constants to build a company that consistently outperforms rivals throughout upturns and downturns.

Step 1: Adopt future-back thinking

This approach entails envisioning a desired future state or outcome and then working backward to the present to determine what actions will be required to realize that future. The focus is on defining an enduring mission and a set of objectives the company can aspire to in any market conditions. Present-forward thinking, in contrast, starts with the current state and looks ahead to the future incrementally. It's more reactive and adaptive, focusing on immediate issues, trends, and competitive pressures. Strategies

developed with a present-forward mindset can change significantly as the company's circumstances evolve.

Future-back thinking helps organizations avoid the pitfalls of
constantly shifting direction in response to every market fluc-
tuation. It encourages businesses to develop a north star that
guides decision-making, investments, and initiatives over an
extended period.

The Netflix transition from DVD-by-mail to streaming exemplifies future-back thinking. As broadband internet became
ubiquitous, Reed Hastings, the CEO of Netflix, spotted a seismic
shift for the video rental industry on the horizon. Despite the
profitability of the DVD-mailing model, he anticipated a future
where streaming video over the internet would predominate.
Advocating for that future, he challenged employees to make
decisions based on what would serve the company's long-term
interests rather than on what would produce short-term gains.

Hastings helped employees understand that the enduring
value offered by Netflix came not from the physical medium of
DVDs but from delivering the best content to customers. The organization recognized that the method of delivery—whether by
mail or streaming—was secondary to the core offering of quality
entertainment. That strategic insight enabled it to pivot effectively and invest in technology that transformed Netflix into a
leading streaming platform.

Step 2: Identify strategic constants

Once companies have envisioned the future, they must solidify
their understanding of the persistent forces driving growth in
their industry. What factors are relevant today and will continue
to be in the future?

The enduring forces can often be evaluated from either a demand or a supply perspective. On the demand side, companies should focus on understanding and addressing the long-standing needs and preferences of their customers. The key is to identify what fundamentally inspires customer choices and loyalty—factors like quality, service, convenience, and brand reputation. Businesses should then tailor their offerings to meet those demands.

Take the retailer Sephora. The chain's strategy hinges on the idea that personalization is a strategic constant in the cosmetics sector. Recognizing that beauty and skin care products suitable for one individual may not work well for another, Sephora has embraced a "try before you buy" ethos. Its stores offer beauty consultations and personalized image-design courses and provide many variations of the same product to meet a wide range of customer preferences.

On the supply side, companies can concentrate on supply chain and operational efficiencies that enable them to deliver their products and services effectively. Supply side constancy emphasizes a firm's operational competencies, including production processes, supply chain management, logistics, and innovation in service delivery.

Unlike other e-commerce giants, China's JD.com has consistently focused on supply chain efficiency and fulfillment excellence, even as the company ventured into new domains and embraced innovative retail formats. JD's tight control over its supply chain has enhanced product quality assurance. As a result, many consumers, despite encountering a broader variety of offerings on other platforms, still prefer JD for their purchases. (Full disclosure: One of us is an adviser to JD.)

Step 3: Match constants to capabilities

This step demands a careful evaluation of a company's intrinsic strengths and the prevailing dynamics of its industry. At organizations in which production excellence, operational efficiency, or technological prowess is a distinguishing capability, a supply side constant may be most appropriate. Conversely, if a firm excels at customer engagement or brand loyalty or possesses a nuanced understanding of market needs, a demand side constant may be the best choice.

Firms should initially anchor their strategies in either demand or supply constants. Because of constraints on resources and management bandwidth, it's difficult to anchor them in both early on. Moreover, strategies focused on one may conflict with strategies focused on the other. Companies pursuing supply chain efficiency, for example, often maintain strict control over their supply chains, sometimes even producing their own products. That can limit their ability to offer a wide range of products.

Amazon resolved those tensions by taking a sequential approach. Initially, it focused on demand side constants like competitive pricing and extensive product variety. But over the years it has also significantly increased its investment in its supply chain, establishing fulfillment centers to serve third-party sellers on its platform and on rival platforms, such as Shopify.

Implementing strategic constancy is not without its challenges. Culturally, a company must embrace the chosen focus. Leaders play a critical role in championing it, ensuring that every major strategic decision reinforces the constancy principle and that the organization is designed to provide the right support and resources.

Step 4: Adapt around the constants

Only once the firm's competitive advantage is firmly rooted in its strategic constants should it consider adaptation. The main goal here is to leverage changes to enhance the advantage provided by the constants. The constants should set the boundaries for the firm's adaptation decisions, including which new businesses to launch and which new technologies to adopt.

Disney has long anchored its strategy in a supply side constant: its extensive portfolio of intellectual properties. These properties underpin the company's film studios, television networks, theme parks, streaming services, and consumer products divisions. In the digital era, Disney has incorporated into its business advanced animation techniques, virtual reality, augmented reality, and interactive entertainment. Those moves have enabled it to create innovative and engaging experiences that expand the appeal of its popular properties in exciting new ways. For example, Disney has developed virtual reality experiences based on *Star Wars* and *The Jungle Book,* allowing users to immerse themselves in the worlds of their favorite characters in novel ways.

Likewise, Sephora, which was renowned for its personalized beauty-shopping experience long before the digital era, has embraced digital transformation by featuring virtual AI-based try-ons both online and in stores and creating an online community focused on beauty topics. Sephora's adoption of technologies has not shifted its focus away from personalized beauty but has instead enhanced its core strength.

. . .

In a rapidly changing environment, companies should establish a firm and consistent strategic foundation rooted in enduring factors while maintaining the flexibility to adapt when necessary. This approach creates both the stability needed to leverage past achievements and the agility needed to evolve. By anchoring strategies in strategic constants, leaders can help their firms navigate uncertainty and ensure that current investments maintain the company's relevance in the long term, reinforcing competitive advantages both now and in the future.

Originally published in November–December 2024. Reprint R2406J

Strategy in a Hyperpolitical World

by Roger L. Martin and Martin Reeves

Almost everything about business today is political, in the sense that it requires consideration of a wide range of often controversial ethical, social, and ecological issues. Choices that may have been clear-cut in purely economic terms—such as what business to be in, where to do business, whom to do business with, and even how to price goods or hire and promote employees—can now easily become complicated by politics.

The stakes for skillfully managing this situation are higher than ever. When Delta stopped offering discounts to NRA members following a 2018 school shooting in Florida, it was threatened with the withdrawal of fuel subsidies in Georgia. When Disney spoke up on LGBTQ+ rights in Florida, it lost its special governance status and rights in the state. When H&M voiced concerns about cotton sourcing and human rights in China, its revenues in that country plummeted. When the Ukraine crisis broke, McDonald's was forced to exit the business it had pains-takingly built in Russia over a 30-year period.

The assumption that business and politics can and even should be separate is no longer realistic—especially where values, identity, and security are concerned. And these days it's not enough to attempt to defuse political issues when they arise by relying on messaging from the corporate affairs department.

What has changed?

Technology has created a new degree of transparency. Companies can no longer manage political tensions by talking and behaving differently to different audiences at different times. In an age when people "bowl alone," the workplace has become the main vehicle for socialization and self-expression. As employees seek to express their identities and beliefs at work, they increasingly expect that their companies will support the issues they care about. It is notable that many CEOs who have taken a stance on social issues say the impetus was that their employees expected and lobbied for it.

At the same time, societies have become more divided, both in opinion and in substance. Inequalities of wealth and income are now more obvious in many countries, generating differences of interest and opinion that are rapidly picked up and amplified on social media. And as economic integration across societies with very different political models, religious beliefs, and values has intensified, new fault lines have appeared, especially between the established nations of the OECD and rising powers such as China.

For business, the result is a web of often conflicting political issues. Backlash can come from a variety of stakeholders. At Google, for example, employees protested the company's proposed censor-friendly Chinese search engine. At H&M the company's Chinese customers opposed its environmental stance. And the backlash

Idea in Brief

The Situation

Recent cultural and economic changes have compelled companies to reassess the values that drive their institutional strategies. Across industries and sectors they are urgently asking themselves what they stand for.

The Challenge

Companies are also realizing that they need to better understand and support the values of their employees. Many have discovered that when they can't align their institutional values with those of their employees, they flounder.

The Solution

In this article the authors provide a method for achieving values alignment by following a five-step process.

may be felt at home for action abroad (Google), abroad for appeals to home values (H&M), or at home for actions that simultaneously appeal to some and inflame others (Delta and Disney).

So what does that mean for strategy?

We define strategy as the art of making informed choices in a competitive environment. Choices are important when differing paths lead to differential risks and rewards. When the social environment is broadly favorable to business, a company's strategic choices can be justified in purely business terms or, as necessary, finessed with carefully crafted press releases. Today, however, choices must be made on an expanded playing field. They are often complex because the underlying ethical, social, and political issues are constantly evolving and defy simple analysis. To make and implement the best strategic choices in this environment, leaders will have to (1) develop robust principles to guide strategic choices, (2) address ethical issues early, (3) consistently communicate and implement their choices, (4) engage beyond the industry to shape the context, and (5) learn from mistakes to make better choices in the future.

Let's examine what those actions involve.

Develop Robust Principles

The aspects of business that can become politicized, and the ways in which that can occur, are so numerous that you can't foresee every challenge. Even some companies that invest in scenario planning failed to predict the Russian invasion of Ukraine. But you should try to anticipate the challenges that are most likely to touch your operations and devise principles that will address them.

Such principles are especially helpful for navigating ethical and political issues that, unlike analytic questions in finance or marketing, are often nuanced and cannot be easily quantified. It was not possible to quantify either the anger of Disney employees over Florida legislation limiting discussion of LGBTQ+ issues in schools (known as the "Don't Say Gay" bill) or the hostility of Florida's Republican governor, Ron DeSantis, in response to Disney's statement on the issue.

Moreover, unique solutions can rarely be deduced for ethical issues, which always involve a judgment call. If your values haven't been codified in a set of principles, it is impossible to choose a reasonable course of action from the facts of the situation alone. What's more, the most complex issues are almost always the most controversial and divisive ones—within a company as well as in the outside world. Having well-thought-through and agreed-upon principles can help minimize the undue politicization and emotional polarization of discussions within the company.

Those principles must be comprehensive enough to apply across the major sources of political tension to which a company is likely to be exposed. For example, they should be appropriate in all jurisdictions, not just straightforward and familiar ones. They should be clear enough to guide choices. "Never commit or condone bribery" is simple and clear. "Do no evil" and "Contribute to societal well-being" are not. And principles should be tangible enough to determine whether they have been applied or not. Tesla's commitment to open-sourcing its patents in the interest of a "common, rapidly evolving technology platform" to fight climate change can be audited easily and objectively.

To develop such principles, the first step is understanding the salient social and political issues for your company. The second step is envisioning where and how those issues might intersect with your business and the choices that they imply. The third step is hearing and understanding the opinions of your employees on those issues—because, as we've noted, they are often the reason that companies take a position on political issues.

Once they've considered these factors, companies can articulate the principles that will guide their choices about where and how to do business. The principles can be tested by predicting where they might realistically prevent you from doing something and what the resulting costs would be over different time periods.

Consider Starbucks, which operates 34,000 stores worldwide in 83 markets and accounts for more than 3% of the global coffee trade. Its segments include at-home coffee, ready-to-drink, and food service channels. Although the company's scale is monumental, its sourcing is localized, encompassing 400,000 farmers in 30 countries across Central America, South America, Africa, and Southeast Asia. In sourcing its beans, Starbucks makes countless business decisions, including which farms to work with, what environmental standards and labor practices to set, how to pay farmers, and what benefits to provide to their communities.

Historically, market forces drove such decisions, but Starbucks and its competitors came under increasing pressure to consider other factors in their sourcing activities. So in 2004 Starbucks decided to codify its commitment to ethical sourcing standards, becoming the first in the coffee industry to do so. The company collaborated with Conservation International to develop the Coffee and Farmer Equity (C.A.F.E.) Practices, which set economic, social, and environmental standards for its sourcing program.

The principles in C.A.F.E., such as "Permanent and temporary/seasonal workers must be paid at least the nationally or regionally established minimum legal wage on a regular basis," are clear, values-informed, and achievable. Each principle comes with explicit policies for enforcement, and a third party monitors farm verification and adherence, flagging shortfalls when they occur. By proactively establishing C.A.F.E. and moving swiftly to correct noncompliance, Starbucks motivated its supplier network to improve practices and transformed reports of abuse from potential public catastrophes into evidence of its commitments writ large.

New principles will serve to guide future business decisions and may very well require immediate changes to company operations if they conflict with prior ones. A commitment to them means that the company will make the principled rather than the commercially expedient choice when required. To be sure, predicting the future perfectly is not possible. But investing in the thought process can reduce the incidence of unanticipated issues and rushed ad hoc decisions.

Address Ethical Issues Early

Just as a company assesses where to operate on the basis of markets' potential attractiveness, evolving trends, and expected competitors' moves, it now also needs to anticipate, preempt, and shape nascent ethical challenges. That may require a high degree of creative problem-solving, but it often garners outsize public goodwill and strategic advantages for early movers. Once an issue has become front-page news, political camps will be entrenched, and the company's room for maneuver will be limited.

Anticipating and shaping ethical challenges requires a delicate balancing act. Individual companies may be able to move earlier and with greater control, but eventually complex issues may necessitate collective action, often initiated by a market leader. Sometimes a combination of collective and individual initiatives can build momentum, influence the issue, and offer advantages of differentiation for the initiator.

In the early 2000s the diamond-mining giant De Beers, like other leaders in its industry, faced a potentially existential crisis. Human rights groups were sounding the alarm on "conflict diamonds"—stones sourced from rebel-controlled regions where they were often mined using inhumane practices or slave labor, with the proceeds going to finance brutal wars. Although they accounted for less than 5% of the world's supply of diamonds and were recovered from countries other than those where De Beers mined, these "blood diamonds" had the potential to tarnish the reputation of the entire industry, erode consumer confidence, and result in a full-scale boycott.

The moral imperative and the business imperative were both clear. De Beers moved swiftly to communicate how it would ensure that it sourced and sold only conflict-free diamonds. But the long value chain from mine to finger and a sophisticated smuggling network presented the risk that illicit diamonds would enter the global supply chain. Safeguarding the industry and ensuring customer confidence would require unique solutions.

De Beers worked with others in the industry and with the UN to establish the Kimberley Process for international certification of conflict-free diamonds. But De Beers went further: It developed a more comprehensive suite of standards—its Best Practice Principles—to address a range of supply chain risks and differentiated itself strategically as "best in industry" for diamond provenance. That involved actions such as limiting diamond sourcing to company-owned mines and developing Tracr, the world's only distributed diamond blockchain, to provide an immutable record of a gem's provenance. This solution, first implemented in 2018, uses artificial intelligence, the internet of things, and advanced security and privacy technologies to enable De Beers to provide assurance not only of a diamond's origins but also of the company's positive impact on the people and places involved in its supply chain (supported by its Building Forever sustainability framework).

De Beers is again leveraging its position to protect the industry and reinforce its brand by spearheading a campaign to expand the definition of conflict diamonds, thus extending the scope of the Kimberley Process, and to cover a wider range of supply chain risks. Meanwhile, it is using Tracr to provide provenance information to the many customers who seek additional assurance in light of sanctions on diamonds from Russia.

Consistently Communicate and Implement Choices

Principles will often collide with reality in either the day-to-day operations or the future planning of an organization and should therefore be communicated to and understood by all employees. Because they will influence the expectations of stakeholders outside the company, they should also be publicly transparent.

However, leaders should not use a megaphone to communicate. The aim is not to provoke, confront, or embarrass but rather to convey what guides the company's decision-making and to reduce future disconnects and surprises. Disney did itself no favors by using a megaphone in its tussle with DeSantis. Its strong statement may have appealed to Disney employees, but it acted as a dramatic provocation for the governor.

Principles are credible only if they are consistently applied. So they must be part of the everyday making of business decisions, not simply called up in response to pressure after a situation has exploded. Navigating the political dimensions of business is hard enough without also having to explain and remedy inconsistent communication or application. And principles that mainly inform communications but not action will not be credible over time or effective in navigating risk.

In applying a company's principles, the aim should not be to judge stakeholders and situations at arm's length. Rather, it should be to engage with and solve issues preemptively and collaboratively whenever possible. A company standing against corruption will have a greater impact if it works with other stakeholders to address that issue and improve the context—even if, at the end of the day, a decision about whether to stay in the business in question or exit it is required.

Since exit or disengagement is by design a possible outcome, orderly exit options should be prepared for, along with clear communication regarding why the company is stepping away. There should always be a plan B for when principles are breached. And exiting is not necessarily inconsistent with continuing to work collaboratively on an underlying issue or with reengaging when the situation has improved.

CVS Health, which includes the U.S. pharmacy chain CVS, provides a good example of getting communication and implementation right. Historically, chains like CVS, Walgreens, and Rite Aid have been community resources: Local residents use them to pick up not only medications but also household essentials—toilet tissue, detergent, stationery—and even cigarettes and alcohol in some places. Over the past decade, however, they have increasingly served as health care providers—administering flu shots, providing basic care, monitoring for chronic conditions, and more. As the chains' health services proliferated, harmful tobacco products sitting on the shelf grew more conspicuous, pitting corporate principles against the bottom line—an opportunity ripe for public outrage.

In February 2014, CVS became the first national pharmacy chain to address this conflict by ending the sale of tobacco products—a decision that would result in an annual revenue loss of $2 billion. But for the company's leaders, removing tobacco was an imperative beyond sales: It was essential to enacting their public principles consistently.

CVS's key competitors took partial measures—raising the minimum age to buy tobacco products to 21 but continuing to sell them—and faced increasing public scrutiny as a result. CVS avoided that scrutiny and used its action as a catalyst for the successful transformation into a health care company. In

September 2014 CVS rebranded as CVS Health; in 2018 it acquired Aetna; and throughout the pandemic it stepped up as a key access point for Covid-19 testing and vaccines. The company's president and CEO, Karen S. Lynch, says, "We have rebuilt and continue to rebuild ourselves as a health care company with a clear purpose of 'Bringing our heart to every moment of your health.'"

Engage Beyond the Industry

There are limits to the power that companies can exercise individually or even in cooperation with competitors, and they will often need to work with civil society and government on the hardest and most deeply entrenched issues to effect change. Therefore they should actively participate in existing solution forums and where necessary help create new ones. The costly alternative is accepting the unpredictability of an endless series of ad hoc responses or having regulation forced on the industry owing to insufficient impact from their own efforts. And there are important new issues around which to build consensus. Applications of AI are a case in point. Over the past decade AI hiring algorithms have become ubiquitous: Now 99% of *Fortune* 500 companies rely on software to sift through job applicants, and 55% of HR leaders in the United States use predictive algorithms in the hiring process.

But controversy has surrounded the rise of AI-based hiring systems, as a lack of external regulation and limited industry-driven standards have allowed them to introduce bias and produce discriminatory outcomes. After all, algorithms reflect the intentions and biases of their architects and the data used to train them. Without careful design and transparency about outcomes, they can become a major source of friction.

In the face of this nascent political issue, Pymetrics, a vendor of algorithm-based hiring software, has sought to change the industry from the inside and preemptively lobbied to bring about regulation. In November 2021 Pymetrics banded together with other software vendors, civil society groups, and corporate users of the software and worked with the city of New York to pass the first law in the nation setting standards for the unbiased use of AI in hiring. In the view of Frida Polli, the CEO of Pymetrics, shaping the discussion and self-regulating were essential for the health of the industry and her own company: "Consumers are losing faith in tech, and there is a real threat of others' imposing legislation if we don't act to bring it about ourselves. Everyone, our company included, loses when tech perpetuates bias."

Learn from Mistakes

Even if you have the best intentions and analysis, political and social issues are intrinsically complex and unpredictable, making surprises and missteps inevitable. When they occur, it's important to extract and incorporate lessons and leverage crises to good effect. In our discussions with company executives, we found that some of the most devoted saints were reformed sinners whose transformations had been catalyzed by public scandal.

For the electrical-engineering giant Siemens, the watershed moment came when an international investigation revealed that the company had paid $1.4 billion in bribes to government officials in Asia, Africa, Europe, the Middle East, and the Americas over several decades. Siemens was brought to account and faced intense public criticism. But it used that moment as the impetus for initiating sweeping internal change.

Siemens began by cleaning house: It hired the company's first-ever external CEO, Peter Löscher, who, within months of taking over, had replaced about 80% of the top level of executives, 70% of the next level down, and 40% of the level below that. Next, it made earnest and long-term commitments to atone for its past actions: It has supported government investigations and set up the global Siemens Integrity Initiative to fund collective action to reduce corruption, which has allowed the company to continue to bid for government contracts. As of July 2021 the initiative's portfolio included 85 projects in more than 50 countries, with funding of nearly $120 million committed.

Finally, and most important, Siemens used the scandal to transform its culture and increase its nimbleness. In Löscher's words, "Never miss the opportunities that come from a good crisis—and we certainly didn't miss ours. The scandal created a sense of urgency without which change would have been much more difficult to achieve." He and his team refocused the business, removed management layers, and altered how the managing board made decisions, thereby resetting the system of control that had enabled the scandal while repositioning the company for market success. (For details, see "The CEO of Siemens on Using a Scandal to Drive Change," HBR, November 2012.)

. . .

We anticipate that with the continued rise of China, instability on Europe's doorstep, and escalating economic and social polarization, the intersection of politics and business will become more fraught. It is time to accept and embrace politics as part of strategic choice and to build the tools and capabilities required to do so. But CEOs must not confuse themselves with politicians or moral watchdogs. Instead they must focus on what is within their purview, albeit in a new context. They must steward the credibility, trustworthiness, and vitality of their enterprises by appreciating the broader and longer-term forces at work in their environment. And they must use what they learn about those forces to make informed choices, to communicate and implement them consistently, and to proactively engage with other actors to shape the context in which they do business.

Originally published in November–December 2022. Reprint S22062

What You Lose with Your New Priorities

by Natalia Weisz and Roberto Vassolo

W hy do organizational strategies so frequently fall short? This question has perennially stumped executives and managers, and one thing seems certain: It's not for lack of planning.

Countless hours are spent by company leaders thinking about, discussing, and planning their strategies. However, several studies have found that about two-thirds of business executives report their planning process does not deliver a robust strategy.[1] In exploring the reasons why, we often hear executives say that the failure of strategic initiatives is due to unpredictable changes in the competitive context—big, unforeseen events and trends. But from our research and work with companies large and small all over the world, we have come to a straightforward conclusion: Unpredictability is over-faulted.[2] On the contrary, we have found that organizations more typically fail at anticipating and then navigating changes that are fairly predictable, having to do with enduring, repeated challenges. Furthermore, there is one key factor that strategic decision-makers often neglect in formulating and implementing their strategies: the crucial role and impact of *loss*.

Hidden Priorities and Losses

We have seen a strong correlation between the failure of strategic initiatives and what we call the "hidden P&L," for priorities and losses. Moving ahead on big, new priorities inevitably generates losses: Some parts of the organization—some people, functions, values, and traditions—will be downgraded or even abandoned in the name of progress. Corporations trying to implement strategic initiatives typically trumpet the benefits and ignore these losses, treating implementation as a straightforward technical challenge. Doing so is a comfortable default. It gives strategic change the illusion of a win-win: No one gets hurt, and nothing gets left behind.

It's a risky, even dangerous illusion. At its best, strategic planning involves informed conversations about the organization's future, resulting in a plan that reflects new priorities or the reordering of old ones. For any strategy to be successful, executives need to identify, understand, and allocate time, attention, energy, and money for the losses the organization will face in pursuit of its new priorities. In this way, strategic planning can be seen as what Ron Heifetz, Marty Linsky, and Alexander Grashow have called an "adaptive challenge," helping the organization come to terms with new realities and appropriately grieve what is lost.[3]

This adaptive challenge can be contrasted with mere "technical" work, in which the factors are known and people continue in the same basic system and circumstances. This means bringing into the strategy-planning process all the tools and frameworks that help teams and organizations deal with the losses that are

Idea in Brief

The Challenge

When organizations implement new strategies, executives often overlook the potential losses associated with the changes, such as valuable aspects of the old strategy that contributed to past successes.

The Solution

Leaders should conduct a thorough analysis of both the gains and the losses associated with a new strategy, such as how it will affect employees' power, income, prestige, career prospects, and autonomy. Engaging stakeholders in this process can help mitigate resistance and foster a more balanced transition.

The Payoff

By acknowledging and addressing the potential losses, organizations can achieve a more holistic and effective implementation. This approach helps maintain continuity, leverages existing strengths, and enhances the overall success of the strategic shift.

part and parcel of doing adaptive work, and actively engaging those people for whom solutions will need to be internalized in minds, commitments, and behaviors.

Dealing with Direct and Indirect Loss

New strategic priorities require organizational changes. We all embrace change when we think it is going to be good for us. What we resist is loss. The latent and often unarticulated fear of loss is usually behind organizational inertia and resistance. Therefore, in any strategic-planning process, it is essential to understand the relationship between the new priorities the context demands and the losses different groups within the organization will face when addressing these priorities.

Some types of losses are clear to detect and eventually address. For example, direct losses relating to power, money, prestige, career prospects, and autonomy come up quickly in planning conversations. More hidden are the competency losses. The fear of having to deal with new organizational demands can trigger significant anxiety. The pain associated with this real or perceived loss of competence can equal or even exceed that of direct losses. We still recall a manager at a major bank saying, "I'm 50 years old, and I don't know whether I can develop the necessary skills for the changes to come." No one wishes to feel incompetent. However, adaptive challenges demand both experimentation and new competencies. They require endurance through painful periods of uncertainty generated by lack of knowledge and relevant skills. Digital transformation in banking creates losses that are a big hurdle for those who have been in the industry for many years.

Loss of loyalty is another serious consideration. No person is an island. We have loyalties to those who share our values, interests, or history. If you serve as a voice for coworkers or friends, then they expect you to defend certain values and perspectives. Upsetting those expectations can carry a high cost, mainly in terms of identity and a sense of belonging. A fear of eroding trust inhibits open conversations about the real work to be done. It undermines progress in strategic priorities.

Such losses are not evenly distributed, and they affect groups differently, varying in type and magnitude. That explains the different levels of commitment and resistance to priorities. The good news is that, just as you can anticipate new priorities in the face of a changing context, you can also anticipate the losses that those priorities will generate.

Building an Adaptive Strategic-Planning Process

Understanding the relationship between priorities and losses can help senior management teams make strategic-planning processes more effective in mobilizing learning and change. Here are three steps you can take to facilitate it.

Strengthen the holding environment

A holding environment is a safe space where executives can talk openly about what they don't know and need to learn, and where the deeper values that will be brought into play during this process can be made explicit. Without a minimum holding environment, the chances of true learning decrease and it becomes more difficult to form an adequate strategy with a coherent set of priorities.

You may never achieve the perfect holding environment, but you can nurture it until it is good enough. Do this by first showing, in a caring way, genuine conviction in addressing the real challenges and the demands they imply. Next, create some temporal and spatial boundaries. Knowing that certain issues must be resolved within a certain time and space helps with focus. Finally, foster emotional connection. For example, people who have been working on the management team for years may actually know less about their peers' histories, hopes, and fears than you might think. This emotional disconnect makes it challenging to show vulnerability and in turn progress in collective learning. One of our favorite ways to strengthen the holding environment is to establish an initial moment for sharing personal stories. Before getting into the corporate needs, we invite managers to learn more from each other by sharing some intimate aspects of their past and present.

Establish a formal moment to discuss losses

Remember that systems, including organizations, can develop the capacity to handle all kinds of challenges—but only those they can name. What we do not recognize and name will later emerge in numerous forms of resistance. So leaders need to make this naming a formal step or goal. While priorities are discussed and agreed upon, the conversation must move from the purely analytic elements of strategy to putting real names and faces to those who would have to implement, manage, and bear the consequences of the decisions resulting from a deep planning process. Inevitably, some of those names and faces also belong to the senior management team and their direct reports. In this sense, beginning to treat strategy as adaptive work humanizes it, enabling the teams to consider the needs and fears of those who must be involved in realizing strategic change. This might be an uncomfortable moment, but it can also be relieving or even freeing if you foster curious questions and deep listening.

Map the affected groups and losses for each strategic priority

As part of the implementation phase, develop a separate picture or chart for each strategic priority, placing it in the center and surrounding it with the most critical groups affected by it. For each group, analyze the extent to which it is involved in the advancement of the adaptive challenge: how members contribute, what is essential for them to preserve, and finally, what they will need to leave behind due to its constraint on their forward motion. You might not have a complete grasp of what all of these aspects imply.

For example, if one of your strategic priorities is to "accelerate digital transformation," then write this initiative in the center of the map and recognize five or six groups or units that will be most affected by the transformation. List for each group the perspective members hold regarding the initiative and the values that underlie that perspective. Then evaluate their commitment and the direct, capability, and loyalty losses they may need to cope with. If you are the senior authority of the organization, don't forget to include yourself on that map. What are the losses you need to acknowledge? What is the learning you need to achieve?

Finally, through the entire process remain close to people and provide interpersonal support. This does not mean solving people's problems, though you may want to. As a leader, you may be able to solve some of the technical issues that strategic change requires, but the real work is more adaptive. Strategic priorities demand deep systemic and individual learning. Fears must be confronted, deep-rooted values will have to be redefined, and behaviors and attitudes will have to change. The basic truth: The people facing the challenge must be part of the solution.

By treating strategic planning as a leadership intervention, you can help people through this process. Adopting an adaptive perspective may not be easy, but ultimately it is more caring and effective.

Adapted from hbr.org, July 13, 2022. Reprint. H074OP

9

Turning Great Strategy into Great Performance

by Michael Mankins and Richard Steele

Three years ago, the leadership team at a major manu-facturer spent months developing a new strategy for its European business. Over the prior half-decade, six new competitors had entered the market, each deploying the latest in low-cost manufacturing technology and slashing prices to gain market share. The performance of the European unit—once the crown jewel of the company's portfolio—had deteriorated to the point that top management was seriously considering divesting it.

To turn around the operation, the unit's leadership team had recommended a bold new "solutions strategy"—one that would leverage the business's installed base to fuel growth in after-market services and equipment financing. The financial forecasts were exciting—the strategy promised to restore the business's industry-leading returns and growth. Impressed, top management quickly approved the plan, agreeing to provide the unit with all the resources it needed to make the turnaround a reality.

Today, however, the unit's performance is nowhere near what its management team had projected. Returns, while better than before, remain well below the company's cost of capital. The revenues and profits that managers had expected from services and financing have not materialized, and the business's cost position still lags behind that of its major competitors.

At the conclusion of a recent half-day review of the business's strategy and performance, the unit's general manager remained steadfast and vowed to press on. "It's all about execution," she declared. "The strategy we're pursuing is the right one. We're just not delivering the numbers. All we need to do is work harder, work smarter."

The parent company's CEO was not so sure. He wondered: Could the unit's lackluster performance have more to do with a mistaken strategy than poor execution? More important, what should he do to get better performance out of the unit? Should he do as the general manager insisted and stay the course—focusing the organization more intensely on execution—or should he encourage the leadership team to investigate new strategy options? If execution was the issue, what should he do to help the business improve its game? Or should he just cut his losses and sell the business? He left the operating review frustrated and confused—not at all confident that the business would ever deliver the performance its managers had forecast in its strategic plan.

Talk to almost any CEO, and you're likely to hear similar frustrations. For despite the enormous time and energy that goes into strategy development at most companies, many have little

Idea in Brief

Most companies' strategies deliver only 63% of their promised financial value. Why? Leaders press for better execution when they really need a sounder strategy. Or they craft a new strategy when execution is the true weak spot.

How to avoid these errors? View strategic planning and execution as inextricably linked—then raise the bar for both simultaneously. Start by applying seven deceptively straightforward rules, including: keeping your strategy simple and concrete, making resource-allocation decisions early in the planning process, and continuously monitoring performance as you roll out your strategic plan.

By following these rules, you reduce the likelihood of performance shortfalls. And even if your strategy still stumbles, you quickly determine whether the fault lies with the strategy itself, your plan for pursuing it, or the execution process. The payoff? You make the right midcourse corrections—promptly. And as high-performing companies like Cisco Systems, Dow Chemical, and 3M have discovered, you boost your company's financial performance 60% to 100%.

.

to show for the effort. Our research suggests that companies on average deliver only 63% of the financial performance their strategies promise. Even worse, the causes of this strategy-to-performance gap are all but invisible to top management. Leaders then pull the wrong levers in their attempts to turn around performance—pressing for better execution when they actually need a better strategy, or opting to change direction when they really should focus the organization on execution. The result: wasted energy, lost time, and continued underperformance.

But, as our research also shows, a select group of high-performing companies have managed to close the strategy-to-performance gap through better planning *and* execution. These companies—Barclays, Cisco Systems, Dow Chemical, 3M, and Roche, to name a few—develop realistic plans that are solidly

Where the performance goes

This chart shows the average performance loss implied by the importance ratings that managers in our survey gave to specific breakdowns in the planning and execution process.

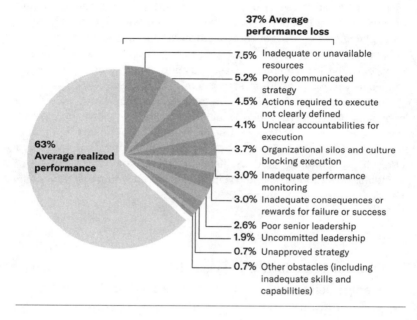

37% Average performance loss

63% Average realized performance

- 7.5% Inadequate or unavailable resources
- 5.2% Poorly communicated strategy
- 4.5% Actions required to execute not clearly defined
- 4.1% Unclear accountabilities for execution
- 3.7% Organizational silos and culture blocking execution
- 3.0% Inadequate performance monitoring
- 3.0% Inadequate consequences or rewards for failure or success
- 2.6% Poor senior leadership
- 1.9% Uncommitted leadership
- 0.7% Unapproved strategy
- 0.7% Other obstacles (including inadequate skills and capabilities)

grounded in the underlying economics of their markets and then use the plans to drive execution. Their disciplined planning and execution processes make it far less likely that they will face a shortfall in actual performance. And if they do fall short, their processes enable them to discern the cause quickly and take corrective action.

While these companies' practices are broad in scope—ranging from unique forms of planning to integrated processes for deploying and tracking resources—our experience suggests that they can be applied by any business to help craft great plans and turn them into great performance.

The Strategy-to-Performance Gap

In the fall of 2004, our firm, Marakon Associates, in collaboration with the Economist Intelligence Unit, surveyed senior executives from 197 companies worldwide with sales exceeding $500 million. We wanted to see how successful companies are at translating their strategies into performance. Specifically, how effective are they at meeting the financial projections set forth in their strategic plans? And when they fall short, what are the most common causes, and what actions are most effective in closing the strategy-to-performance gap? Our findings were revealing—and troubling.

While the executives we surveyed compete in very different product markets and geographies, they share many concerns about planning and execution. Virtually all of them struggle to produce the financial performance forecasts in their long-range plans. Furthermore, the processes they use to develop plans and monitor performance make it difficult to discern whether the strategy-to-performance gap stems from poor planning, poor execution, both, or neither. Specifically, we discovered:

Companies rarely track performance against long-term plans

In our experience, less than 15% of companies make it a regular practice to go back and compare the business's results with the performance forecast for each unit in its prior years' strategic plans. As a result, top managers can't easily know whether the projections that underlie their capital-investment and portfolio-strategy decisions are in any way predictive of actual performance. More important, they risk embedding the same disconnect between results and forecasts in their future investment decisions. Indeed, the fact that so few companies routinely monitor actual versus planned performance may help explain why so many companies seem to pour good money after bad—continuing to fund losing strategies rather than searching for new and better options.

Multiyear results rarely meet projections

When companies do track performance relative to projections over a number of years, what commonly emerges is a picture one of our clients recently described as a series of "diagonal venetian blinds," where each year's performance projections, when viewed side by side, resemble venetian blinds hung diagonally. (See the exhibit "The venetian blinds of business.") If things are going reasonably well, the starting point for each year's new "blind" may be a bit higher than the prior year's starting point, but rarely does performance match the prior year's projection. The obvious implication: year after year of underperformance relative to plan.

The venetian blinds phenomenon creates a number of related problems. First, because the plan's financial forecasts are unreliable, senior management cannot confidently tie capital approval to strategic planning. Consequently, strategy development and resource allocation become decoupled, and the annual operating plan (or budget) ends up driving the company's long-term investments and strategy. Second, portfolio management gets derailed. Without credible financial forecasts, top management cannot know whether a particular business is worth more to the company and its shareholders than to potential buyers. As a result, businesses that destroy shareholder value stay in the portfolio too long (in the hope that their performance will eventually turn around), and value-creating businesses are starved for capital and other resources. Third, poor financial forecasts

The venetian blinds of business

This figure illustrates a dynamic common to many companies. In January 2001, management approves a strategic plan (Plan 2001) that projects modest performance for the first year and a high rate of performance thereafter, as shown in the first solid line. For beating the first year's projection, the unit management is both commended and handsomely rewarded. A new plan is then prepared, projecting uninspiring results for the first year and once again promising a fast rate of performance improvement thereafter, as shown by the second solid line (Plan 2002). This, too, succeeds only partially, so another plan is drawn up, and so on. The actual rate of performance improvement can be seen by joining the start points of each plan (the dotted line).

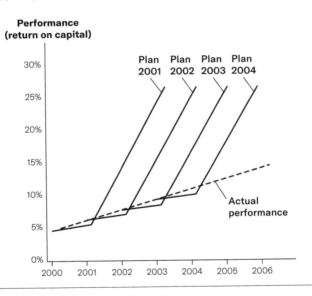

complicate communications with the investment community. Indeed, to avoid coming up short at the end of the quarter, the CFO and head of investor relations frequently impose a "contingency" or "safety margin" on top of the forecast produced by consolidating the business-unit plans. Because this top-down contingency is wrong just as often as it is right, poor financial forecasts run the risk of damaging a company's reputation with analysts and investors.

A lot of value is lost in translation

Given the poor quality of financial forecasts in most strategic plans, it is probably not surprising that most companies fail to realize their strategies' potential value. As we've mentioned, our survey indicates that, on average, most strategies deliver only 63% of their potential financial performance. And more than one-third of the executives surveyed placed the figure at less than 50%. Put differently, if management were to realize the full potential of its current strategy, the increase in value could be as much as 60% to 100%!

As illustrated in the exhibit "Where the performance goes," the strategy-to-performance gap can be attributed to a combination of factors, such as poorly formulated plans, misapplied resources, breakdowns in communication, and limited accountability for results. To elaborate, management starts with a strategy it believes will generate a certain level of financial performance and value over time (100%, as noted in the exhibit). But, according to the executives we surveyed, the failure to have the right resources in the right place at the right time strips away some 7.5% of the strategy's potential value. Some 5.2% is lost to poor communications, 4.5% to poor action planning, 4.1% to blurred accountabilities, and so on. Of course, these estimates reflect the average experience of the executives we surveyed and may not be representative of every company or every strategy. Nonetheless, they do highlight the issues managers need to focus on as they review their companies' processes for planning and executing strategies.

What emerges from our survey results is a sequence of events that goes something like this: Strategies are approved but poorly communicated. This, in turn, makes the translation of strategy into specific actions and resource plans all but impossible. Lower levels in the organization don't know what they need to do, when they need to do it, or what resources will be required to deliver the performance senior management expects. Consequently, the expected results never materialize. And because no one is held responsible for the shortfall, the cycle of underperformance gets repeated, often for many years.

Performance bottlenecks are frequently invisible to top management

The processes most companies use to develop plans, allocate resources, and track performance make it difficult for top management to discern whether the strategy-to-performance gap stems from poor planning, poor execution, both, or neither. Because so many plans incorporate overly ambitious projections, companies frequently write off performance shortfalls as "just another hockey-stick forecast." And when plans are realistic and performance falls short, executives have few early-warning signals. They often have no way of knowing whether critical actions were carried out as expected, resources were deployed on schedule, competitors responded as anticipated, and so on. Unfortunately, without clear information on how and why performance is falling short, it is virtually impossible for top management to take appropriate corrective action.

The strategy-to-performance gap fosters a culture of underperformance

In many companies, planning and execution breakdowns are reinforced—even magnified—by an insidious shift in culture. In our experience, this change occurs subtly but quickly, and once it has taken root it is very hard to reverse. First, unrealistic plans create the expectation throughout the organization that plans simply will not be fulfilled. Then, as the expectation becomes experience, it becomes the norm that performance commitments won't be kept. So commitments cease to be binding promises with real consequences. Rather than stretching to ensure that commitments are kept, managers, expecting failure, seek to protect themselves from the eventual fallout. They spend time covering their tracks rather than identifying actions to enhance performance. The organization becomes less self-critical and less intellectually honest about its shortcomings. Consequently, it loses its capacity to perform.

Closing the Strategy-to-Performance Gap

As significant as the strategy-to-performance gap is at most companies, management can close it. A number of high-performing companies have found ways to realize more of their strategies' potential. Rather than focus on improving their planning and execution processes separately to close the gap, these companies work both sides of the equation, raising standards for both planning and execution simultaneously and creating clear links between them.

Our research and experience in working with many of these companies suggests they follow seven rules that apply to planning and execution. Living by these rules enables them to objectively assess any performance shortfall and determine whether it stems from the strategy, the plan, the execution, or employees' capabilities. And the same rules that allow them to spot problems early also help them prevent performance shortfalls in the first place. These rules may seem simple—even obvious—but when strictly and collectively observed, they can transform both the quality of a company's strategy and its ability to deliver results.

Rule 1: Keep it simple, make it concrete

At most companies, strategy is a highly abstract concept—often confused with vision or aspiration—and is not something that can be easily communicated or translated into action. But without a clear sense of where the company is headed and why, lower levels in the organization cannot put in place executable plans. In short, the link between strategy and performance can't be drawn because the strategy itself is not sufficiently concrete.

To start off the planning and execution process on the right track, high-performing companies avoid long, drawn-out descriptions of lofty goals and instead stick to clear language describing their course of action. Bob Diamond, CEO of Barclays Capital, one of the fastest-growing and best-performing investment banking operations in Europe, puts it this way: "We've been very clear about what we will and will not do. We knew we weren't going to go head-to-head with U.S. bulge bracket firms. We communicated that we wouldn't compete in this way and that we wouldn't play in unprofitable segments within the equity markets but instead would invest to position ourselves for the euro, the burgeoning need for fixed income, and the end of Glass-Steigel. By ensuring everyone knew the strategy and how it was different, we've been able to spend more time on tasks that are key to executing this strategy."

By being clear about what the strategy is and isn't, companies like Barclays keep everyone headed in the same direction. More important, they safeguard the performance their counterparts lose to ineffective communications; their resource and action planning becomes more effective; and accountabilities are easier to specify.

Rule 2: Debate assumptions, not forecasts

At many companies, a business unit's strategic plan is little more than a negotiated settlement—the result of careful bargaining with the corporate center over performance targets and financial forecasts. Planning, therefore, is largely a political process—with unit management arguing for lower near-term profit projections (to secure higher annual bonuses) and top management pressing for more long-term stretch (to satisfy the board of directors and other external constituents). Not surprisingly, the forecasts that emerge from these negotiations almost always understate what each business unit can deliver in the near term and overstate what can realistically be expected in the long term—the hockey-stick charts with which CEOs are all too familiar.

Even at companies where the planning process is isolated from the political concerns of performance evaluation and compensation, the approach used to generate financial projections often has built-in biases. Indeed, financial forecasting frequently takes place in complete isolation from the marketing or strategy functions. A business unit's finance function prepares a highly detailed line-item forecast whose short-term assumptions may be realistic, if conservative, but whose long-term assumptions are largely uninformed. For example, revenue forecasts are typically based on crude estimates about average pricing, market growth, and market share. Projections of long-term costs and working capital requirements are based on an assumption about annual productivity gains—expediently tied, perhaps, to some companywide efficiency program. These forecasts are difficult for top management to pick apart. Each line item may be completely defensible, but the overall plan and projections embed a clear upward bias—rendering them useless for driving strategy execution.

High-performing companies view planning altogether differently. They want their forecasts to drive the work they actually do. To make this possible, they have to ensure that the assumptions underlying their long-term plans reflect both the real economics of their markets and the performance experience of the company relative to competitors. Tyco CEO Ed Breen, brought in to turn the company around in July 2002, credits a revamped plan-building process for contributing to Tyco's dramatic recovery. When Breen joined the company, Tyco was a labyrinth of 42 business units and several hundred profit centers, built up over many years through countless acquisitions. Few of Tyco's businesses had complete plans, and virtually none had reliable financial forecasts.

To get a grip on the conglomerate's complex operations, Breen assigned cross-functional teams at each unit, drawn from strategy, marketing, and finance, to develop detailed information on the profitability of Tyco's primary markets as well as the product or service offerings, costs, and price positioning relative to the competition. The teams met with corporate executives biweekly during Breen's first six months to review and discuss the findings. These discussions focused on the assumptions that would drive each unit's long-term financial performance, not on the financial forecasts themselves. In fact, once assumptions about market trends were agreed on, it was relatively easy for Tyco's central finance function to prepare externally oriented and internally consistent forecasts for each unit.

Separating the process of building assumptions from that of preparing financial projections helps to ground the business unit–corporate center dialogue in economic reality. Units can't hide behind specious details, and corporate center executives can't push for unrealistic goals. What's more, the fact-based discussion resulting from this kind of approach builds trust between the top team and each unit and removes barriers to fast and effective execution. "When you understand the fundamentals and performance drivers in a detailed way," says Bob Diamond, "you can then step back, and you don't have to manage the details. The team knows which issues it can get on with, which it needs to flag to me, and which issues we really need to work out together."

Rule 3: Use a rigorous framework, speak a common language

To be productive, the dialogue between the corporate center and the business units about market trends and assumptions must be conducted within a rigorous framework. Many of the companies we advise use the concept of profit pools, which draws on the competition theories of Michael Porter and others. In this framework, a business's long-term financial performance is tied to the total profit pool available in each of the markets it serves and its share of each profit pool—which, in turn, is tied to the business's market share and relative profitability versus competitors in each market.

In this approach, the first step is for the corporate center and the unit team to agree on the size and growth of each profit pool. Fiercely competitive markets, such as pulp and paper or commercial airlines, have small (or negative) total profit pools. Less competitive markets, like soft drinks or pharmaceuticals, have large total profit pools. We find it helpful to estimate the size of each profit pool directly—through detailed benchmarking—and then forecast changes in the pool's size and growth. Each business unit then assesses what share of the total profit pool it can realistically capture over time, given its business model and positioning. Competitively advantaged businesses can capture a large share of the profit pool—by gaining or sustaining a high market share, generating above-average profitability, or both. Competitively disadvantaged businesses, by contrast, typically capture a negligible share of the profit pool. Once the unit and the corporate center agree on the likely share of the pool the business will capture over time, the corporate center can easily create the financial projections that will serve as the unit's road map.

In our view, the specific framework a company uses to ground its strategic plans isn't all that important. What is critical is that the framework establish a common language for the dialogue between the corporate center and the units—one that the strategy, marketing, and finance teams all understand and use. Without a rigorous framework to link a business's performance in the product markets with its financial performance over time, it is very difficult for top management to ascertain whether the financial projections that accompany a business unit's strategic plan are reasonable and realistically achievable. As a result, management can't know with confidence whether a performance shortfall stems from poor execution or an unrealistic and ungrounded plan.

Rule 4: Discuss resource deployments early

Companies can create more realistic forecasts and more executable plans if they discuss up front the level and timing of critical resource deployments. At Cisco Systems, for example, a cross-functional team reviews the level and timing of resource deployments early in the planning stage. These teams regularly meet with John Chambers (CEO), Dennis Powell (CFO), Randy Pond (VP of operations), and the other members of Cisco's executive team to discuss their findings and make recommendations. Once agreement is reached on resource allocation and timing at the unit level, those elements are factored into the company's two-year plan. Cisco then monitors each unit's actual resource deployments on a monthly basis (as well as its performance) to make sure things are going according to plan and that the plan is generating the expected results.

Challenging business units about when new resources need to be in place focuses the planning dialogue on what actually needs to happen across the company in order to execute each unit's strategy. Critical questions invariably surface, such as: How long will it take us to change customers' purchase patterns? How fast can we deploy our new sales force? How quickly will competitors respond? These are tough questions. But answering them makes the forecasts and the plans they accompany more feasible.

What's more, an early assessment of resource needs also informs discussions about market trends and drivers, improving the quality of the strategic plan and making it far more executable. In the course of talking about the resources needed to expand in the rapidly growing cable market, for example, Cisco came to realize that additional growth would require more trained engineers to improve existing products and develop new features. So rather than relying on the functions to provide these resources from the bottom up, corporate management earmarked a specific number of trained engineers to support growth in cable. Cisco's financial-planning organization carefully monitors the engineering head count, the pace of feature development, and revenues generated by the business to make sure the strategy stays on track.

Rule 5: Clearly identify priorities

To deliver any strategy successfully, managers must make thousands of tactical decisions and put them into action. But not all tactics are equally important. In most instances, a few key steps must be taken—at the right time and in the right way—to meet planned performance. Leading companies make these priorities explicit so that each executive has a clear sense of where to direct his or her efforts.

At Textron, a $10 billion multi-industrial conglomerate, each business unit identifies "improvement priorities" that it must act upon to realize the performance outlined in its strategic plan. Each improvement priority is translated into action items with clearly defined accountabilities, timetables, and key performance indicators (KPIs) that allow executives to tell how a unit is delivering on a priority. Improvement priorities and action items cascade to every level at the company—from the management committee (consisting of Textron's top five executives) down to the lowest levels in each of the company's ten business units. Lewis Campbell, Textron's CEO, summarizes the company's approach this way: "Everyone needs to know: 'If I have only one hour to work, here's what I'm going to focus on.' Our goal deployment process makes each individual's accountabilities and priorities clear."

The Swiss pharmaceutical giant Roche goes as far as to turn its business plans into detailed performance contracts that clearly specify the steps needed and the risks that must be managed to achieve the plans. These contracts all include a "delivery agenda" that lists the five to ten critical priorities with the greatest impact on performance. By maintaining a delivery agenda at each level of the company, Chairman and CEO Franz Humer and his leadership team make sure "everyone at Roche understands exactly what we have agreed to do at a strategic level and that our strategy gets translated into clear execution priorities. Our delivery agenda helps us stay the course with the strategy decisions we have made so that execution is actually allowed to happen. We cannot control implementation from HQ, but we can agree on the priorities, communicate relentlessly, and hold managers accountable for executing against their commitments."

Rule 6: Continuously monitor performance

Seasoned executives know almost instinctively whether a business has asked for too much, too little, or just enough resources to deliver the goods. They develop this capability over time—essentially through trial and error. High-performing companies use real-time performance tracking to help accelerate this trial-and-error process. They continuously monitor their resource deployment patterns and their results against plan, using continuous feedback to reset planning assumptions and reallocate resources. This real-time information allows management to spot and remedy flaws in the plan and shortfalls in execution—and to avoid confusing one with the other.

At Textron, for example, each KPI is carefully monitored, and regular operating reviews percolate performance shortfalls—or "red light" events—up through the management ranks. This provides CEO Lewis Campbell, CFO Ted French, and the other members of Textron's management committee with the information they need to spot and fix breakdowns in execution.

A similar approach has played an important role in the dramatic revival of Dow Chemical's fortunes. In December 2001, with performance in a free fall, Dow's board of directors asked Bill Stavropoulos (Dow's CEO from 1993 to 1999) to return to the helm. Stavropoulos and Andrew Liveris (the current CEO, then COO) immediately focused Dow's entire top leadership team on execution through a project they called the Performance Improvement Drive. They began by defining clear performance metrics for each of Dow's 79 business units. Performance on these key metrics was tracked against plans on a weekly basis, and the entire leadership team discussed any serious discrepancies first thing every Monday morning. As Liveris told us, the weekly monitoring sessions "forced everyone to live the details of execution" and let "the entire organization know how we were performing."

Continuous monitoring of performance is particularly important in highly volatile industries, where events outside anyone's control can render a plan irrelevant. Under CEO Alan Mulally, Boeing Commercial Airplanes' leadership team holds weekly business performance reviews to track the division's results against its multiyear plan. By tracking the deployment of resources as a leading indicator of whether a plan is being executed effectively, BCA's leadership team can make course corrections each week rather than waiting for quarterly results to roll in.

Furthermore, by proactively monitoring the primary drivers of performance (such as passenger traffic patterns, airline yields and load factors, and new aircraft orders), BCA is better able to develop and deploy effective countermeasures when events throw its plans off course. During the SARS epidemic in late 2002, for example, BCA's leadership team took action to mitigate the adverse consequences of the illness on the business's operating plan within a week of the initial outbreak. The abrupt decline in air traffic to Hong Kong, Singapore, and other Asian business centers signaled that the number of future aircraft deliveries to the region would fall—perhaps precipitously. Accordingly, BCA scaled back its medium-term production plans (delaying the scheduled ramp-up of some programs and accelerating the shutdown of others) and adjusted its multiyear operating plan to reflect the anticipated financial impact.

Rule 7: Reward and develop execution capabilities

No list of rules on this topic would be complete without a reminder that companies have to motivate and develop their staffs; at the end of the day, no process can be better than the people who have to make it work. Unsurprisingly, therefore, nearly all of the companies we studied insisted that the selection and development of management was an essential ingredient in their success. And while improving the capabilities of a company's workforce is no easy task—often taking many years—these capabilities, once built, can drive superior planning and execution for decades.

For Barclays' Bob Diamond, nothing is more important than "ensuring that [the company] hires only A players." In his view, "the hidden costs of bad hiring decisions are enormous, so despite the fact that we are doubling in size, we insist that as a top team we take responsibility for all hiring. The jury of your peers is the toughest judgment, so we vet each others' potential hires and challenge each other to keep raising the bar." It's equally important to make sure that talented hires are rewarded for superior execution. To reinforce its core values of "client," "meritocracy," "team," and "integrity," Barclays Capital has innovative pay schemes that "ring fence" rewards. Stars don't lose out just because the business is entering new markets with lower returns during the growth phase. Says Diamond: "It's so bad for the culture if you don't deliver what you promised to people who have delivered. . . . You've got to make sure you are consistent and fair, unless you want to lose your most productive people."

Companies that are strong on execution also emphasize development. Soon after he became CEO of 3M, Jim McNerney and his top team spent 18 months hashing out a new leadership model for the company. Challenging debates among members of the top team led to agreement on six "leadership attributes"— namely, the ability to "chart the course," "energize and inspire others," "demonstrate ethics, integrity, and compliance," "deliver results," "raise the bar," and "innovate resourcefully." 3M's leadership agreed that these six attributes were essential for the company to become skilled at execution and known for accountability. Today, the leaders credit this model with helping 3M to sustain and even improve its consistently strong performance.

. . .

The prize for closing the strategy-to-performance gap is huge— an increase in performance of anywhere from 60% to 100% for most companies. But this almost certainly understates the true benefits. Companies that create tight links between their strategies, their plans, and, ultimately, their performance often experience a cultural multiplier effect. Over time, as they turn their strategies into great performance, leaders in these organizations become much more confident in their own capabilities and much more willing to make the stretch commitments that inspire and transform large companies. In turn, individual managers who keep their commitments are rewarded—with faster progression and fatter paychecks—reinforcing the behaviors needed to drive any company forward.

Eventually, a culture of overperformance emerges. Investors start giving management the benefit of the doubt when it comes to bold moves and performance delivery. The result is a performance premium on the company's stock—one that further rewards stretch commitments and performance delivery. Before long, the company's reputation among potential recruits rises, and a virtuous circle is created in which talent begets performance, performance begets rewards, and rewards beget even more talent. In short, closing the strategy-to-performance gap is not only a source of immediate performance improvement but also an important driver of cultural change with a large and lasting impact on the organization's capabilities, strategies, and competitiveness.

Originally published in July–August 2005. Reprint R0507E

10

Bringing True Strategic Foresight Back to Business

by Amy Webb

recently sat down with the CEO of a large corporation, who asked a peculiar question: Would I rather have a crystal ball that always showed me the future or a chessboard that always told me the right strategy? He's a sharp, curious thinker who likes to debate—but on this day, he was mulling an urgent problem.

While the company was the undisputed leader among its competitors, the CEO was growing concerned about outside disrupters. He worried that his leadership team wasn't thinking broadly enough about how the macro forces shaping society would eventually impact the business landscape. Managers weren't surfacing bold, new ideas, and amid all the uncertainty brought by artificial intelligence, inflation, and the post-Covid workforce, they weren't willing to take strategic risks.

Meanwhile, the company had become adept at strategy execution—testing competitor responses, selecting new technology vendors, building certain capabilities—but they were only chasing incremental wins. Throughout the company, managers weren't willing to use foresight to plan beyond a few quarters, fearing that any decisions made today could be wrong tomorrow.

The CEO pressed me to debate him. Which is better? The ability to see the future or the ability to create and execute the right strategy? There is a clear answer, I told him. Strategy and foresight were once the same discipline. And they should be again.

How Strategy and Foresight Disconnected

In the 1980s and 1990s, forward-looking companies used strategy and foresight together as a powerful dual force that guided leaders to peer over the horizon with data-backed, quantitative models; compelling narratives about plausible futures; and informed choices to stay competitive. The goal was to provide a defensible long-term point of view, align on key themes, and engage leaders in a common dialogue about multiple scenarios for the future.

At the same time, leaders and managers alike would use that foresight base to create, calibrate, and execute their near-term strategies. They had a shared perspective on where and how to grow, how to execute new positions, and how to maintain and defend the core business.

Over time, however, strategy and foresight diverged into separate disciplines. In the 1990s, companies started adding strategy professionals, sometimes called chief strategy officers (CSOs), to

Idea in Brief

The Problem

In the past, many organizations used strategy and foresight as parallel disciplines, creating a long-term, data-backed point of view that guided leaders to peer over the horizon. Today, though, strategy and foresight are often handled separately, making the latter too far removed from actual business needs to wield real influence.

The Solution

Executives should reunite strategy and foresight, recognizing that they operate on the same continuum and resetting expectations for what they can achieve together. Adopting modern tools and techniques to enhance future-oriented thinking and fostering a culture that values long-term planning can embed strategic foresight as a core competency.

The Payoff

By reintegrating foresight into strategic planning, leaders can better anticipate disruptions, identify opportunities, make informed decisions that ensure organizational resilience, and ensure they aren't taking a limited, too-narrow view of the future.

their management teams. CSOs were often hired from consulting firms, and they were charged with developing winning strategies along with tactics and operations to ensure effective decision-making and execution.

As the C-suite delegated more initiatives to CSOs and their teams, strategy managers, strategic planners, business analysts, and others wound up doing less strategy work. These days, I see CSOs often serving as a proxy for their CEOs, while their teams do everything from taking the lead on executing priority initiatives to finding attractive new markets. Meanwhile, foresight, which used to involve quantitative data, predictive modeling, behavioral insights, and storytelling to craft intricate scenarios designed to prepare companies for multiple future states, has devolved into company speeches, workshops, and lightweight scenarios that lack rigor. In my observation, foresight output is now too far removed from the actual business needs of the company to wield real influence.

As strategy and foresight drifted onto separate paths, companies lost the synergy that originally made each discipline so potent. Just like other iconic duos you already know—Simon and Garfunkel, Kirk and Spock, Sherlock and Watson—strategy and foresight are better together, because they amplify what each element could achieve alone. Strategy without foresight makes companies vulnerable to outside disruption. Foresight without strategy renders scenarios unactionable. Each on its own has value, but our current business environment demands both.

It's time to reunite strategy and foresight, recognize that they operate on the same continuum, and reset expectations for what they can achieve together. With modern updates and improvements to these combined disciplines, leaders can sharpen their vision for the future, empowering managers to make informed strategic choices and propelling teams toward superior performance. This domain is true *strategic foresight*: a disciplined and systematic approach to identify where to play, how to win in the future, and how to ensure organizational resiliency in the face of unforeseen disruption.

We are in the most challenging operating environment I've seen in 20 years, and this moment demands a new mindset. Within the corporate setting, executives I meet with are curious about strategic foresight, but they treat it like a buzzword and aren't yet clear on its value. This article aims to define strategic foresight for leaders, advocating for its integration as a core competency in every organization, regardless of size.

Why Corporate Strategy
Needs Updating

Corporate strategy is crucial for establishing a sustainable competitive edge, yet it is increasingly failing to drive the long-term growth it once promised. I see the original purpose of corporate strategy as creating a long-term plan for developing a business's competitive advantage and then compounding it. At best, corporate strategy is an opportunity to define a company's near-term competitive and operational plans and also helm its long-term research and visioning.

I rarely see this in practice today. What's happened is that executives ask for long-term strategic perspectives, but in reality they are limiting their teams to narrow time frames, resulting in a perpetual review of the same objectives with only minor adjustments. Here's a sobering truth that most C-suites won't acknowledge: Considering the speed at which most modern companies are reasonably capable of moving (read: laboriously slow compared with the rate of external change), by the time a two-year plan is executed the future will have moved further out of reach. Strategy's mission-critical responsibility—to chart a clear organizational direction and follow through with a robust execution plan—is being overridden by the immediate pressures of resource allocation and everyday operational tactics.

Many CSOs I know feel trapped. They wind up with ambiguous, all-encompassing mandates: Act as CEO whisperer, provide support for board-level engagement, facilitate stakeholder management, and serve as a Jane-of-all-trades, special-projects person. As a result, CSOs find themselves both responsible for everything and accountable for nothing, since the results reside with the business owners or managers within the company.

I remember sitting down with the CSO of a leading consumer-packaged goods (CPG) company grappling with an outdated margin-management approach, focused solely on cost-cutting and ranging from packaging redesigns to operational shifts such as plant relocations. The intent was to reinvest these savings into innovation to propel the company into a new growth phase. Yet the strategy team's preoccupation with margin improvements overshadowed the drive for innovation, causing the company to miss research-backed opportunities and leaving it exposed to market disruption.

This underscores a wider problem faced by many companies: While managing margins is vital, it must be balanced with the pursuit of innovation and growth opportunities to prevent strategic myopia and secure a company's competitive edge in the future. When strategy isn't performing its intended job, companies can't continually improve, leverage disruptive technologies, and adapt to new market conditions.

The immediacy of day-to-day operations can lead to a strategic process that is more about ticking boxes and filling templates, which often end up languishing, unopened, in an inbox. Today's tactical actions must set the course for the desired future, but the desired future must be regularly reevaluated as dynamics change to make sure the intended destination hasn't shifted.

The Promise and Peril of Corporate Foresight

The promise of corporate foresight is that it will position leaders to make good decisions in times of deep, soul-crushing uncertainty. And that's the peril: The way foresight is practiced today doesn't typically yield data-backed recommendations to guide leaders on new-market expansion, M&A strategy, innovation road maps, sustainability efforts, or the myriad other initiatives they prioritize. The foresight function is often positioned inside a research or marketing team, where outputs aren't tied specifically to strategic outcomes. Foresight teams within organizations tend to lack formal training in how to build quantitative models or how to calculate the trajectory and momentum of trends. They also lack the direct profit and loss accountability that business heads typically hold. These days, foresight must do more than change the perspectives of a company's leaders. It must drive business results.

Foresight, like other business disciplines, is both an art and a science, but without a standard methodology and set of tools it's rendered ambiguous or even unexplainable to nonpractitioners. Even among practitioners, there is little consensus on what exactly a "trend" is and how that's different from a "strong signal" or a "macro trend" or a "force." Some people call themselves "futurists," while others hate that term, and still others use different descriptors, such as "insights" or "forecaster," to describe what they do. ("Strategy" may sound generic, but at least it's just one word.) Foresight also performs different functions depending on the industry. Foresight teams in CPG companies target emerging trends for near-term product strategies, while in insurance, the focus is on long-term risks for future profitability and product line responses.

Second, the output of corporate foresight teams is undermined by a lack of rigor in methodology and an overreliance on subject-matter-expert interviews, internal surveys, and secondary sources. A common complaint I hear from executives is that the output of a foresight team's work—most often trend reports and scenarios—fails to land due to weak research, the lack of quantitative models, and too heavy a reliance on a few expert opinions.

I recall a meeting I had with the CEO and CFO of a telecommunications company, who were presented with M&A recommendations that stemmed from an internal foresight team's trend report. To the company's leaders (and frankly to me as well), the recommendations were too broad, obvious, and outdated. The team had worked for months to deliver fresh insights to leadership, so what happened? There was no methodology. Instead, they'd aggregated third-party research and interviewed their usual experts.

Contemporary foresight suffers from the template-ification of trend reports and scenarios, leading to bias and missed opportunities. One popular approach involves prioritizing two or three topics of interest to a leadership team and writing iterations of scenarios after workshops and individual or group discussions. The goal is alignment on main ideas, and it typically results in confirmation bias instead of fresh insights.

A third reason foresight fails to achieve impact in companies is straightforward: People aren't willing to say they make predictions. If they tell a CEO that the scenario is a "forecast, not a prediction," it undermines their perceived relevance to business strategy and creates confusion among the stakeholders they aim to inform and persuade. Ultimately, a scenario *is* a form of prediction—a deeply researched preview of how the world might unfold. The details of a prediction can and will change from time to time, because the world isn't static. The goal isn't to be right or wrong but to refine the strategic actions that should drive the company forward, even when every variable can't be controlled.

How to Operationalize Strategic Foresight in Your Organization

Putting strategy and foresight back together results in assessing potential futures, managing the strategic pivots necessary to navigate them, and crucially, measuring the efficacy of such initiatives. This triad—assessment, management, and measurement—is the backbone of effective strategic foresight and is what brings the best of both together. Strategic foresight is inherently interdisciplinary, not multidisciplinary. Which means that the leader or team should not be siloed.

Strategic foresight should be given a cross-functional reach, and the team's mandate should be to interact with and provide services and support to multiple segments of the organization. For that reason, strategic foresight should be horizontally positioned, working with different units (such as marketing, finance, operations, and product development) to ensure that the company collectively knows where to play and how to win, and crucially, that it will be prepared to adapt in uncertain business climates. New strategic foresight teams, with business unit involvement, should align on a repeatable methodology that can produce actionable insights, competitive strategy, and strategy execution capable of achieving business goals and objectives set by leadership.

My approach to strategic foresight, which we use at the Future Today Institute and which I teach at NYU Stern School of Business, is rooted in deep research and rigorous modeling, game theory and strategy, and storytelling. Here's an overview of our 10-step process:

1. *Signal detection.* Combine primary research, expert insights, and AI-driven pattern recognition to detect early signals of change, bypassing traditional horizon scanning for a continuous, data-rich approach.

2. *Trend identification.* Measure trends using momentum, trajectory, and disruptive potential, assigning scores based on quantitative data such as market activity and regulatory shifts.

3. *Macro themes.* Identify overarching themes by prioritizing trends with significant data-driven impact, leading to strategic dialogues with leadership.

4. *Uncertainties.* Address the unpredictable by categorizing uncertainties, and prioritize them to cover a wide strategic range. Use STREEEP+W: social, technological, regulatory, environmental, economic, ethical, political, and wild cards.

5. *Develop hypotheses about the future.* Generate broad hypotheses by combining trends and uncertainties, drawing on tools such as the 2 × 2 matrix and the Monte Carlo simulation—a powerful automated statistical technique that uses variables to model a range of possible outcomes—to minimize bias.

6. *Scenarios.* Scenarios should be put together specifically for the executive, manager, or team using them to make decisions, and they should always be backed by research. In our work, we don't use a standard template, because the culture of every organization is very different.

7. *Bridge to strategy.* Use scenarios to perform a SWOT analysis (strengths, weaknesses, opportunities, and threats), challenging assumptions and testing the organization's adaptability to future conditions.

8. *Strategy.* Use traditional strategic planning to align stakeholders and gain executive buy-in, focusing on key decisions like product development and M&A.

9. *Strategy execution.* Align organizational roles with strategic goals, establish new performance metrics, and execute operational tactics.

10. *Measure and recalibrate.* Teams should institute a way to continuously monitor progress and be able to make agile adjustments to tactics in response to real-time market feedback and evolving business landscapes.

While the overall process is linear, there is no end to this work. Teams should maintain a cycle of strategic foresight through continuous signal detection, trend identification, and the development of actionable insights. Our approach is unique and specific—but effective. While every strategic foresight team should adopt and formalize its own repeatable method, it absolutely must be anchored in research, modeling, storytelling, and strategy.

Strategic Foresight in Practice

Strategic foresight can position any company to survive and thrive amid uncertainty. Here's how this might work for a bank facing the uncertainty of AI. Say emerging trends point to a future where smart home appliances become the norm, along with innovative decentralized marketplaces for computing power. These marketplaces, leveraging peer-to-peer protocols, allow users to connect with and pay each other for sharing their unused resources. Our demand for computing resources continues to skyrocket, putting a strain on providers. One plausible scenario: Households generate computing power for those who need it and earn money from their smart TVs, washing machines, and mobile devices while they're not being used. Banks could become a trusted intermediary, facilitating both the secure peer-to-peer network and payments between parties, charging a nominal fee. This is a novel opportunity for banks to play and win by reframing AI as infrastructure.

Netflix transitioned from DVD rentals to streaming services, preempting the shift in consumer habits toward online content consumption—a move that has cemented its market dominance. Schibsted, an Oslo-based portfolio of digital consumer brands (and a company we advise), used strategic foresight to anticipate how the internet might crush its advertising business and drew on those insights to create its own digital advertising business. Today, Schibsted is one of the most successful and respected media companies in the world.

We've counseled insurance executives to develop a long-term strategy on underwriting and investment bank CEOs to guide their M&A in challenging areas such as AI. We've used our strategic foresight methodology to help CPG companies to know what products to create, hotel companies to understand what digital infrastructure to invest in, and pharmaceutical companies to prioritize which therapeutics to pursue next. Each of these examples underscores how strategic foresight—when correctly applied—can create a competitive edge and a buffer against the inevitable forces of disruption, well into the future.

We live in a far more complex world today than corporate strategists and futurists ever envisioned. Leaders, forget your crystal balls and your chessboards. Strategic foresight is effective, it's within your reach, and it will help you navigate the next waves of disruption and transformation.

Adapted from hbr.org, January 12, 2024. Reprint H07ZB4

Discussion Guide

Are you feeling inspired by what you've read in this collection? Do you want to share the ideas in the articles or explore the insights you've gleaned with others? This discussion guide offers an opportunity to dig a little deeper, with questions to prompt personal reflection and to start conversations with your team.

You don't need to have read the book from beginning to end to use this guide. Choose the questions that apply to the articles you have read or that you feel might spark the liveliest discussion.

Reflect on key takeaways from your reading to help you adopt the ideas and techniques you want to integrate into your work as a leader. What tools can you share with your team to help everyone be their best? Becoming the leader you want to be starts with a detailed plan—and a commitment to carrying it out.

1. In chapter 1 Michael Porter explains the five forces that shape competitive strategy: threat of new entrants, bargaining power of suppliers, bargaining power of buyers, threat of substitute products or services, and industry rivalry. What are some examples of how these forces currently affect your industry and company? How might they affect your company differently in the future, and why?

2. What are some potential blue oceans—areas where your company can create uncontested market space—in your industry? What strategic moves could your organization take to prevent competitors from finding success in those areas?

3. How can your company ensure that its strategic choices, such as Where to Play and How to Win, are made so that they reinforce each other? How could leaders better align these kinds of strategic choices across different levels of the company?

4. In your own words, what is your organization's core purpose? Has it changed over time? How could the purpose be better woven into your strategy, products, and services?

5. What's an example of how cognitive biases—such as relying on intuition more than data, or overestimating the chances of success—influenced your decisions in the past? How could you reduce these biases' impact in the future?

6. What are the warning signs in your industry that a source of advantage is fading and it's time to find a new one? How could your company build more flexibility into its strategy-setting processes so that leaders can adjust their goals and objectives when that happens?

7. How has the rise of AI affected your company's strategic positioning? What challenges or unknowns are preventing the organization from taking fuller advantage of AI's capabilities?

8. What ecosystems is your company part of, and what is your exact role within them? What could the organization do to create and capture more value in these ecosystems?

9. What barriers have gotten in the way of implementing and/or communicating your company's strategy? What makes these barriers so hard to resolve?

10. When has your company fallen victim to the "agility trap" by trying to keep up with every technological advancement, new market dynamic, or shift in consumer preferences? What were the consequences?

11. For politicized situations or issues, what principles or values guide your organization's strategic choices? Which specific situations or issues have been the hardest for your company to navigate, and why?

12. When have you or your team experienced losses (of power, competence, or identity, for example) due to the implementation of a new strategy? What could help you or your team better adapt to new realities and manage the associated changes?

13. What methods does your organization use to systematically identify and evaluate future opportunities and threats? How could the company better align its short-term actions and its long-term vision?

14. What other sources on strategy have had a significant impact on your work? Were there voices or subtopics you missed in this collection? Were there voices or subtopics included that surprised you?

15. After reading and reflecting on this book and discussing it with people on your team, write down the ideas and techniques you want to try. Think of how you might experiment and implement them in both the short term and long term. Draft a plan to move forward.

Notes

Quick Read: Take the Bias Out of Strategy Decisions

1. Robert A. Burgelman, "Fading Memories: A Process Theory of Strategic Business in Dynamic Environments," *Administrative Science Quarterly* 39, no. 1 (March 1994): 24–56.

2. Roger Buehler et al., "Perspectives on Prediction: Does Third-Person Imagery Improve Task Completion Estimates?," *Organizational Behavior and Human Decision Processes* 117, no. 1 (January 2012): 138–149.

Quick Read: What You Lose with New Priorities

1. Mark Judah, Dunigan O'Keeffe, David Zehner, and Lucy Cummings, "Strategic Planning That Produces Real Strategy," Bain & Company, February 2016, https://www.bain.com/insights/strategic-planning-that -produces-real-strategy/.

2. Roberto S. Vassolo and Natalia Weisz, *Strategy as Leadership: Facing Adaptive Challenges in Organizations* (Stanford, CA: Stanford Business Books, 2022).

3. Ronald A. Heifetz, Marty Linsky, and Alexander Grashow, *The Practice of Adaptive Leadership: Tools and Tactics for Changing Your Organization and the World* (Boston, MA: Harvard Business Press, 2009).

About the Contributors

Ivy Buche is a research fellow and term research professor at IMD, in Lausanne, Switzerland.

Charles Dhanaraj is the J. Mack Robinson Professor of International Business and the academic director of the Doctor of Business Administration program at the Robinson School of Business at Georgia State University.

Marco Iansiti is the David Sarnoff Professor of Business Administration at Harvard Business School, where he is a codirector of the Digital Initiative. He is also a codirector of the Laboratory of Information Science at Harvard. He has advised many companies in the technology sector, including Microsoft, Facebook, and Amazon. He is a coauthor (with Karim Lakhani) of the book *Competing in the Age of AI* (Harvard Business Review Press, 2020).

Michael G. Jacobides is the Sir Donald Gordon Professor of Entrepreneurship and Innovation and a professor of strategy at London Business School.

W. Chan Kim is a professor of strategy and management at INSEAD and a codirector of the INSEAD Blue Ocean Strategy Institute, in Fontainebleau, France. He is a coauthor, with Renée Mauborgne, of the books *Blue Ocean Strategy* and *Beyond Disruption* (Harvard Business Review Press, 2005 and 2023, respectively).

Karim R. Lakhani is the Dorothy and Michael Hintze Professor of Business Administration at Harvard Business School, as well as the chair and a cofounder of the Digital, Data, and Design Institute and founder and codirector of the Laboratory for Innovation Science at Harvard University. He is a coauthor (with Marco Iansiti) of *Competing in the Age of AI* (Harvard Business Review Press, 2020).

Jianwen Liao is a professor of strategy and innovation at the Cheung Kong Graduate School of Business and a senior adviser to the chair of JD Group.

Thomas W. Malnight is an emeritus professor of strategy and general management at IMD, in Lausanne, Switzerland.

Michael Mankins is a leader in Bain's Organization Design, Corporate Strategy, and Transformation practices and a partner based in Austin, Texas. He is a coauthor of *Time, Talent, Energy* (Harvard Business Review Press, 2017).

Roger L. Martin is a former dean of the Rotman School of Management, an adviser to CEOs, and the author of *A New Way to Think* (Harvard Business Review Press, 2022).

Renée Mauborgne is a professor of strategy at INSEAD and a codirector of the INSEAD Blue Ocean Strategy Institute, in Fontainebleau, France. She is a coauthor, with W. Chan Kim, of the books *Blue Ocean Strategy* and *Beyond Disruption* (Harvard Business Review Press, 2005 and 2023, respectively).

Rita McGrath is a professor at Columbia Business School and a globally recognized expert on strategy in uncertain and volatile environments. She is the author of *The End of Competitive Advantage* (Harvard Business Review Press, 2013) and *Seeing Around Corners*.

Andrea Belk Olson is a differentiation strategist, speaker, author, and customer-centricity expert. She is the CEO of Pragmadik, a behavioral-science-driven change agency, and has served as an outside consultant for EY and McKinsey. She is the author of three books, a four-time American Advertising Award winner, and a contributing author for *Entrepreneur, Rotman Management Magazine, Chief Executive*, and *Customer Experience Magazine*.

Michael E. Porter is the Bishop William Lawrence University Professor at Harvard Business School. He has served as an adviser to governments and campaigns around the world on the advancement of social policy and economic policy, including Mitt Romney's presidential campaign. He is an academic adviser to the Leadership Now Project.

Martin Reeves is the chairman of Boston Consulting Group's BCG Henderson Institute. He is a coauthor, with Jack Fuller, of *The Imagination Machine* (Harvard Business Review Press, 2021) and a coauthor, with Bob Goodson, of *Like: The Button That Changed the World* (Harvard Business Review Press, 2025).

Richard Steele is a partner at McKinsey & Co., based in New York City.

Roberto Vassolo is a professor of strategic management at IAE Business School. He is the coauthor of *Strategy as Leadership*.

Freek Vermeulen is a professor at London Business School and the author of *Breaking Bad Habits* (Harvard Business Review Press, 2017).

Amy Webb is a quantitative futurist, the CEO of Future Today Institute, and a professor of strategic foresight at the New York University Stern School of Business. She is the author of *The Signals Are Talking*, *The Big Nine*, and *The Genesis Machine*.

Natalia Weisz is a professor of organizational behavior at IAE Business School. She is the coauthor of *Strategy as Leadership*.

Feng Zhu is the MBA Class of 1958 Professor of Business Administration at Harvard Business School. He is a coauthor of *Smart Rivals* (Harvard Business Review Press, 2024).

Index

Work is hard. Let us help.

Engage with HBR content the way you want, on any device.

Whether you run an organization, a team, or you're trying to change the trajectory of your own career, let *Harvard Business Review* be your guide. Level up your leadership skills by subscribing to HBR.

HBR is more than just a magazine—it's access to a world of business insights through articles, videos, audio content, charts, ebooks, case studies, and more.